Impatient Optimist

Also read

I, Steve: Steve Jobs in his own words

Impatient Optimist

BILL GATES

in his own words

Edited by LISA ROGAK

HARPER
BUSINESS

First published in India in 2012 by Collins Business
An imprint of HarperCollins *Publishers*
4th Floor, Tower A, Building No. 10, DLF Cyber City,
DLF Phase II, Gurugram, Haryana – 122002
www.harpercollins.co.in
This edition published in India in 2017 by Harper Business

8 10 9 7

Through arrangement with the Mendel Media Group LLC of New York

P-ISBN: 978-93-5029-384-3
E-ISBN: 978-93-5029-552-6

Typeset in New Baskerville & Univers

Printed and bound at
MicroPrints India, New Delhi

This is how I see the world, and it should make one thing clear: I am an optimist. But I am an impatient optimist.

—*Creative Capitalism*, 2008

CONTENTS

INTRODUCTION

Love him or hate him, Bill Gates has been a venerable worldwide business icon for more than three decades, ever since the first mass-produced personal computer debuted in 1981.

Alternately described as an ingenious visionary and a tyrannical, sometimes less-than-scrupulous businessman, it's been all but impossible to ignore him. But despite their opinion of Gates, even his most prominent naysayers have no choice but to admit the obvious: he helped to spearhead one of the greatest revolutions in modern history by turning the inaccessible computer technology of the 1970s into an invaluable and easy-to-use tool for the masses, while also providing jobs and wealth to many along the way.

Gates has consistently been ranked as one of the world's wealthiest men — as well as one of the most controversial founders and CEOs in history — and businesspeople of all stripes have taken their cues from him, using his words and business strategies to help create and grow their own companies. And in contrast to his hard-nosed reputation, after he left running the day-to-day operations of Microsoft in 2008 to devote himself full time to the Bill & Melinda Gates Foundation, a kinder, gentler side began to emerge. As a result, people who are actively involved in their own philanthropic efforts have begun to take a second look at the man.

Despite the fact that he's no longer at the helm of one of the world's most powerful companies, Gates has steadfastly remained in the news. His friendship and philanthropic partnerships with U2's Bono and investing titan Warren Buffett attract the attention of both the media and the public, which only helps to gain more attention for his charitable acts, whether it's testifying with former US president Bill Clinton about increasing federal aid to earthquake-ravaged cities and villages in Haiti, or making the rounds at the Sundance Film Festival to promote the topic of public education reform. And unlike Gates' days at Microsoft, where he was entrusted with protecting a bevy of corporate secrets, today his life is virtually an open book, featuring regular updates on Facebook and Twitter and blog posts at TheGatesNotes.com.

Bill Gates' second act is no less compelling than his first. Anyone interested in his personal life or looking for inspiration to drive forward their own business endeavours can find enlightenment through reading Gates' own words.

QUOTATIONS

ACQUIRING OTHER COMPANIES

We've done a number of acquisitions in our history ... A lot of the time, the reason we do the acquisition is, when we see a market developing very rapidly ... we want to reduce the amount of time it takes us to get in there, get working with customers, get the feedback that's valuable.

—Keynote speech, San Jose State, 27 January 1998.

ADDICTION TO TECHNOLOGY

If a kid is addicted to a personal computer, I think that's far better than watching TV, because at least his mind is making choices.

—*Programmers at Work*, 1986.

AFRICAN-AMERICAN EDUCATIONAL DISPARITY

It's a great irony that *Brown v. Board of Education* is viewed as a milestone in civil rights, and yet the difference in the quality of what the average black student was getting in 1954 versus what the average student is getting today is not that great ... Some of the more outrageous [segregation laws were] easier to ... solve than this school thing.

—*Ebony*, October 2011.

Why isn't there outrage, absolute outrage over this issue [of disparity in the education system]? Why aren't there protests every day, I don't understand. Why wouldn't this activate people the way that it did during the Civil Rights Movement?

—*Ebony*, October 2011.

AIR TRAVEL

[Flying economy] costs less money. You get there just as fast as flying first class. And my body fits. If I was really wide or really tall, I might view the issue differently.

—*New York Times* News Service/Syndicate, 29 August 1995.

AMERICA

I was a huge beneficiary of this country's unique willingness to take [a] risk on a young person.

—CNBC Town Hall Event, Columbia University, 12 November 2009.

AMERICAN UNIVERSITIES

Our university system is the best. We fund our universities to do a lot of research and that is an amazing thing. We reward risk taking ... It is a chaotic system, but it is a great engine of innovation in the world, and with federal tax money [and] philanthropy on top of that, [it will continue to flourish].

— *The World is Flat*, 2005.

ANALYSING OTHER COMPANIES

We focus on what companies do well as opposed to what they do poorly. We don't dismiss a company as unimportant just because a lot of things about it may be less than perfect. The company may be doing something important; it may not even know that it is important.

— *New York Times* News Service/Syndicate,
19 February 1996.

(HIS) ANTISOCIAL TENDENCIES

... I came to be the leader of the antisocial group [at Harvard]. We clung to each other as a way of validating our rejection of all those social people.

—Commencement address, Harvard University, 7 June 2007.

ANDY GROVE

Andy Grove is an incredible CEO. He's big on picking objectives, and driving the company towards that objective. He's big on clarity. He is an engineering manager, par excellence.

—KEYNOTE SPEECH, SAN JOSE STATE, 27 JANUARY 1998.

ANTI-VACCINE PROPONENTS

It's an absolute lie that has killed thousands of kids. Because the mothers who heard that lie, many of them didn't have their kids take either pertussis or measles vaccine[s], and their children are dead today. And so the people who go and engage in those anti-vaccine efforts, they kill children. It's a very sad thing, because these vaccines are important.

—CNN, 4 FEBRUARY 2011.

APPLE

To create a new standard, it takes something that's not just a little bit different; it takes something that's really new, and really captures people's imagination. And the Macintosh — of all the machines I've seen — is the only one that meets that standard.

—SPEECH, 1984.

BAD NEWS

There is a tendency in companies to let good news travel fast. Oh, we just won this account. Oh, things went so well. But, the thing about good news is, it's generally not actionable ... Bad news, on the other hand, is actionable. This customer is not very happy. This competitor is doing something very well. This project is behind ... The sooner you get the bad news, the better off you're going to be, in order to kind of absorb it, to change your product plan, to go back and talk to the people, really dig into it. So when somebody sends me mail saying, you know, we won XYZ account for Exchange, I send mail back and say, does that mean we lost every other account, because you only sent me mail on one account? Tell me about the ones we lost, and why? And so that's really gotten into our culture.

—KEYNOTE SPEECH, SAN JOSE STATE, 27 JANUARY 1998.

BEING CEO

Steve Ballmer said ... that the responsibility of being CEO was more burdensome than he had expected. Well, I told him before he took the job that it was an inhuman job. It makes infinite demands on you, and I feel very lucky that I have Steve. I think he's stepping into the shoes exactly the way I hoped he would.

—*Newsweek*, 16 April 2000.

BEING IN CHARGE

[In high school I told the other programmers], 'Look, if you want me to come back you have to let me be in charge. But this is a dangerous thing, because if you put me in charge this time, I'm going to want to be in charge forever after.'

—Smithsonian Institution Oral and Video Histories, 2003.

BEING THE FACE OF MICROSOFT

Externally, people tend to identify the company with one person. It's a natural thing so I've had mostly the minuses, but [also] the pluses of that.

—*Newsweek*, 23 June 1997.

People's perception of the importance of my role is certainly greater than the reality.

—*Newsweek*, 1 December 1996.

The world has had a tendency to focus a disproportionate amount of attention on me.

—*U.S. News & World Report*, 16 June 2006.

BONO

[One night] he was on fire, talking about how we could get a percentage of each purchase from civic-minded companies to help change the world. He kept calling people, waking them up, and handing me the phone. His projections were a little enthusiastic at first — but his principle was right. If you give people a chance to associate themselves with a cause they care about, they will pay more, and that premium can make an impact.

—SPEECH, 2008 WORLD ECONOMIC FORUM, 24 JANUARY 2008.

I tend to be a little more realistic. [Bono is] always saying, 'Yeah, we can do this!'

— *TIME*, 26 DECEMBER 2005.

It's not about making himself look good. [Bono] really reads this stuff; he cares about the complexity. Look, Bono is really, really having an impact. Things would be very different without him.

— *TIME*, 26 DECEMBER 2005.

BREAKTHROUGHS

A breakthrough is something that changes the behaviour of hundreds of millions of people where, if you took it away from them, they'd say, 'You can't take that away from me.' Breakthroughs are critical for us. All we get paid for are breakthroughs, because people who have our software today can keep using it forever and not pay us another dime.

—*Newsweek*, 24 November 2003.

BUSINESS COMPUTING

[A business's] corporate memory is not very good unless somebody who is working on a project can sit down at their PC and in less than sixty seconds call up any memos or documents that might relate to a similar project that was done in the past. If it takes more time than that, people probably won't go and find it.

—Speech, Enterprise Perspective, 24 March 1999.

BUSINESS CUSTOMERS

Your most unhappy customers are your greatest source of learning.

— *Business @ The Speed of Thought*, 1999.

BUSINESS CUSTOMERS

One thing that never comes out is that the software business is bigger selling to businesses than it is to consumers. Microsoft is really in touch with what are the practicalities, how do you make workers more productive, what are the pains in an IT department, what does corporate site development involve. We have built up over the decades the real ability to have great ongoing dialogue with businesses about how they do their software and what they do. We have a very strong position.

—*PC Magazine*, 25 June 2008.

BUSINESS STANDARDS

I really shouldn't say this, but in some ways it leads, in an individual product category, to a natural monopoly: where somebody properly documents, trains, promotes a particular package and through momentum, user loyalty, reputation, sales force and prices builds a very strong position with that product.

—Rosen Research Personal Computer Forum Proceedings, May 1981.

CAPITALISM

People underestimate how effective capitalism is at keeping even the most successful companies on edge.

— *The Rich & How they Got that Way*, 2001.

Capitalism is great and having thousands of things going on in parallel. And a lot of them fail.

Some are just mediocre. But the ones that are special can grow and, you know, stun everybody.

And in all those fields I mentioned, there [are] going to be several companies that kind of take your breath away.

—CNBC Town Hall Event, Columbia University, 12 November 2009.

CAREER

I've been very lucky. I've had two jobs that were absolutely fantastic. When I was young, writing software, staying up all night, you know, dreaming about the personal computer I wanted and I thought would be great for everyone, that was the perfect thing for me. And now I've switched. I'm totally full time on the foundation. You know, I'm loving advocating for these causes. I'm making sure that the money our foundation spends is — is used in the best way possible … I love doing this work.

—CNN, 20 July 2010.

....

Even today, what interests me isn't making money per se. If I had to choose between my job and having great wealth, I'd choose the job. It's a much bigger thrill to lead a team of thousands of talented, bright people than it is to have a big bank account.

—*New York Times* News Service/Syndicate,
27 October 1996.

CEDING POWER TO BALLMER

I had to change. Steve is all about being on the team, and being committed to the mutual goals. So I had to figure out, what are my behaviours that don't reinforce that? What is it about sarcasm in a meeting? Or just going, 'This is completely screwed up?'

— *The Wall Street Journal*, 5 June 2008.

CHALLENGES

There is a certain irony that somebody says we have this enduring position that's unassailable, like some guy who owns the only copper mine in the world. The truth is very much the opposite. The company faces challenges and we need to pull together as a team and do great work.

— *Newsweek*, 16 April 2000.

CHANGE

Every three years are important in terms of redefining what we do. Any company that stays the same will be passed by very quickly and there are lots of fine examples of that ... Because we now have a research group, and we are out there working with lots of universities and are able to continue to hire great people, I'm very optimistic about our future. But, it is a future full of change and surprise.

—Smithsonian Institution Oral and Video Histories, 2003.

The barrier to change is not too little caring; it is too much complexity.

—Commencement address, Harvard University, 7 June 2007.

CHILDHOOD

I tried to be normal
the best I could.

—*Hard Drive*, 1992.

CHILDHOOD

I really had a lot of dreams when I was a kid, and I think a great deal of that grew out of the fact that I had a chance to read a lot.

—*PC Magazine*, 23 June 2008.

CHINA

About three million computers get sold every year in China, but people don't pay for the software. Someday they will, though. As long as they are going to steal it, we want them to steal ours. They'll get sort of addicted, and then we'll somehow figure out how to collect sometime in the next decade.

—CNET News, 2 July 1998.

It's exciting to see what's going on in China. It's great for us. If we had a choice for all the people in China to be as rich as we are versus be as poor as they were back in 1979, we'd be way better off to say, you know, let's have them be consumers and inventors just like we are. They are a long ways away from that. But they are a large enough population that great things are happening there.

—CNBC Town Hall Event, Columbia University,
12 November 2009.

The Chinese have risk-taking, hard work down, education, and when you meet with Chinese politicians, they are all scientists and engineers. You can have numeric discussion with them — you are never discussing 'give me a one-liner to embarrass [my political rivals] with'. You are meeting with an intelligent bureaucracy.

— *The World is Flat*, 2005.

The Chinese are clearly inculcating the idea that science is exciting and important, and that's why they, as a whole — they're graduating four times as many engineers as we are, and that's just happened over the last twenty years.

— *Morning Edition*, 29 April 2005.

In China when you're one in a million, there are 1300 people just like you.

— *Time*, 13 January 1997.

....

[Today], I would rather be a genius born in China than an average guy born in Poughkeepsie.

— *The World is Flat*, 2005.

CLIMATE CHANGE

But can we, by increasing efficiency, deal with our climate problem? The answer is basically no. The climate problem requires more than a 90 percent reduction in CO_2 emitted, and no amount of efficiency improvement is going to address that. As we're improving our efficiency, poor people are increasing their energy intensity. You're never going to get the amount of CO_2 emitted to go down unless you deal with the one magic metric, which is CO_2 per kilowatt-hour.

— *Wired*, July 2011.

CLONING

I think cloning is a bad thing. And they'll pass regulations that prevent any of that being done on humans in any way.

—*20/20*, 30 JANUARY 1998.

CLOUD COMPUTING

People get confused. There is storage in the cloud, which is clear that your file should be up there and geo-distributed and backed up, and there is computation in the cloud. The one that you have to be careful of is what about computation, because computation is not free. But we are actually taking some pilot customers and moving huge parts of their data centres into our cloud where we manage it for them. Over the next couple of years, a portion of the data centres will start to move. Some people say data centres will move to the cloud very quickly, but I tend to think it will vary a lot.

—*PC MAGAZINE*, 23 JUNE 2008.

COLLEGE EDUCATION

It concerns me to hear young people say they don't want to go to college because I didn't graduate. For one thing, I got a pretty good education even though I didn't stay long enough to get my degree. For another, the world is getting more competitive, specialised and complex each year, making a college education as critical today as a high school education was at one time.

—*New York Times* News Service/Syndicate, 13 May 1996.

COMPETITION

Whether it's Google or Apple or free software, we've got some fantastic competitors and it keeps us on our toes.

—*Telegraph*, 11 February 2010.

All good capitalistic companies get up every morning and think, 'How can we make a better product? What are they doing well? We're going to make it cheaper, better, simpler, faster.'

And great competitors spur companies on. And at every phase of our industry, it's been a different set of companies.

—CNN, 5 October 2008.

We try to understand what other people are doing, even if their apparent mission is so distant that it is not obvious competition.

—*New York Times* News Service/Syndicate, 19 February 1996.

You basically have to convince the other guys not to spend enough money to compete with us, to keep just making it harder and harder, move the terms up, we just keep raising the bar, and eventually maybe one of them will try to do stuff with us. But a lot of them will just say, 'Forget it.'

—*Masters of Enterprise*, 1999.

You always have to be thinking about who is coming to get you.

—*Showstopper!*, 1994.

COMPUTERS VS. PEOPLE

Computers are great because when you're working with them you get immediate results that let you know if your program works. It's feedback you don't get from many other things.

—*The Road Ahead*, 1995.

CONTINUING TO WORK AFTER BECOMING A BILLIONAIRE

I still feel this is superfun.

—*Time*, 13 January 1997.

CONCEPT OF TIME

Measuring time is always tricky when you're someone who is on email night and day.

—*Newsweek*, 30 June 2008.

COOPERATION

I've never done anything solo, except take tests.

—*Working Together*, 2010.

You can't just get a bunch of smart people together and know which path they should go off and pursue. Actually, it's amazing that that worked for the Manhattan Project.

—*Technology Review*, 1 September 2010.

CORPORATE ANTI-DISCRIMINATION POLICY

There is this question on, say, a broad social issue, [do you] take the most controversial ... position? When you have customers, shareholders, employees strongly on both sides of an issue that the company will not take a position on, this one, if it comes up again, we're going to go through a process and, you know, make sure that we're choosing to take a position or not for the right reasons. People can know what we stand for as a company in terms of anti-discrimination. They can also know that we won't necessarily take a position on every social issue that comes up.

—*Morning Edition*, 28 April 2005.

CORPORATE SOCIAL RESPONSIBILITY

It's amazing how strong a message is hidden in words like 'diversity' or the broad term 'corporate social responsibility'. A company needs to have core values of who they are and what they do [which] makes employees feel they have a purpose and guides their action.

— *Creative Capitalism*, 2008.

I'll be the first to admit that it's very easy to make statements about this that sound good ... there's a lot of room for fluffery in this space, and so you've got to bring in expertise and that will probably take a while to develop.

—*Creative Capitalism*, 2008.

CORPORATE STRATEGY

Size works against excellence. Even if we are a big company, we cannot think like a big company or we are dead.

—*Financial Times*, 10 June 1996.

CORPORATE WORKING ENVIRONMENT

I've always believed in a paperless office.

—CNNMoney/*Fortune*, 12 April 1999.

CREATIVITY

We tell people that if no one laughs at at least one of their ideas, they're probably not being creative enough.

—*New York Times* News Service/Syndicate, 9 October 1996.

Generally, creative people like to work with each other. You have to make sure you're encouraging an atmosphere where the creative people feel comfortable, so you get positive momentum. A lot of people here have become very wealthy. We have to keep the place really fun. Otherwise, they have the freedom to go off and do other things.

—*Success Magazine*, October 1988.

CRITICISING EMPLOYEES

Great organisations demand a high level of commitment by the people involved. That's true in any endeavour. I've never criticised a person. I have criticised ideas. If I think something's a waste of time or inappropriate I don't wait to point it out. I say it right away. It's real time. So you might hear me say, That's the dumbest idea I have ever heard many times during a meeting.

—*Playboy*, July 1994.

CRITICS

God, fuck this guy [Philippe Kahn]! I mean, I really hate this guy. I'm so much more technical than that guy is, Jesus Christ!

— *Masters of Enterprise*, 1999.

People are going to second-guess anything you do.

— *Newsweek*, 30 August 1999.

When you have the level of success that we've had, when you have a business that's important as this, with this many competitors, you're going to have people saying some nasty things. And so you have to learn a little bit not to take it too personally.

— *20/20*, 30 January 1998.

If we weren't so ruthless, we'd be making more creative software? We'd rather kill a competitor than grow the market? Those are clear lies. Who grew this market? We did. Who survived companies like IBM, ten times our size, taking us on?

— *Time*, 13 January 1997.

How have things gone since 1995? Have our sales increased? Have our profits increased? (Answer: yes, about tenfold.) Do we also wish we'd done everything that Google has done? Sure. But I'll take our track record since 1995 versus anyone.

—*Newsweek*, 30 June 2008.

DECIDING WHICH PROJECTS TO FUND

Arming myself with knowledge and sitting down with people who live the topic and brainstorming with them, that's what helps me back the right people and make sure I know what's going on.

—CNBC Town Hall Event, Columbia University,
12 November 2009.

....

If you believe that every life has equal value, it's revolting to learn that some lives are seen as worth saving and others are not. We said to ourselves: 'This can't be true. But if it is true, it deserves to be the priority of our giving.'

—Commencement address, Harvard University,
7 June 2007.

DETERMINATION

I can do anything
I put my mind to.

—*Hard Drive*, 1992.

DELEGATING

We were always making the system somewhat more formalised. At some point you can't discuss every head in France and [have] the one guy at the top saying, 'No, no, no. You want fifteen ... you need eleven.' You can't, you just can't, so eventually you have to delegate that.

— *Microsoft Rebooted*, 2004.

DROPPING OUT OF HARVARD

We realised that things were starting to happen, and just because we'd had a vision for a long time of where this chip could go and what it could mean didn't mean the industry was going to wait for us while I stayed and finished my degree at Harvard.

— *Triumph of the Nerds*, June 1996.

EARLY COMPETITORS

There certainly were a lot of other software companies. Within two or three years of our being started, there were dozens of companies. Some of them tried to do better BASIC. And we made darn sure they never came near to what we had done. There were competitors in other languages. They didn't take quite the same long-term approach that we did, doing multiple products, really being able to hire people and train them to come in and do great work, taking a worldwide approach, and thinking of how the various products could work together.

—Smithsonian Institution Oral and Video Histories, 2003.

EARLY COMPUTERS

The early dream was a machine that was easy to use, very reliable and very powerful. We even talked back in 1975 about how we could make a machine that all of your reading and note-taking would be done on that machine.

— *What the Best CEOs Know*, 2005.

EARLY DAYS

We didn't even obey a 24-hour clock, we'd come in and program for a couple of days straight ... four or five of us. When it was time to eat we'd all get in our cars, kind of race over to the restaurant and sit and talk about what we were doing. Sometimes I'd get excited talking about things, I'd forget to eat, but then you know, we'd just go back and program some more. It was us and our friends — those were fun days.

— *Triumph of the Nerds*, June 1996.

Life for us was working and maybe going to a movie and then working some more. Sometimes customers would come in, and we were so tired we'd fall asleep in front of them. Or at an internal meeting I'd lie down on the floor, because I like to do that to brainstorm. And then I'd just fall asleep.

—CNNMoney/*Fortune*, 2 October 1995.

We had contests to see who could stay in the building like three or four days straight. Some of the more prudish people would say, 'Go home and take a bath.'

— *Masters of Enterprise*, 1999.

We thought the world would be like it is now in terms of the popularity and impact of the PC, but we didn't have the hubris to think that our company would be this size or have this kind of success. The paradox is that we thought, 'OK, we can just have this thirty-person company that will be turning out the software for every PC.'

—*Newsweek*, 17 September 2000.

I was the mover. I was the guy who said, 'Let's call the real world and try to sell something to it.'

—*Hard Drive*, 1992.

If you had asked me at any point how big Microsoft could be, Paul [Allen] and I once thought we could write all the software in the world with 100 people. If you had told us that someday we would have more than 5000 people writing software, we would have just shaken our heads.

—CNNMoney/*Fortune*, 2 October 1995.

E-BOOKS

I read a lot of obscure books and it is nice to open a book. But the electronic devices are good as well. Digital reading will completely take over. It's lightweight and it's fantastic for sharing. Over time it will take over.

—Mail Online, 12 June 2011.

ECONOMIC CRISIS

The case studies of this crisis will be taught for decades to come. At least we'll get that benefit out of the pain we went through. Leverage is a very dangerous thing. Warren [Buffett] has talked about derivatives as weapons of mass destruction. That wasn't much heeded ... And the mass destruction followed as predicted.

—CNBC Town Hall Event, Columbia University,
12 November 2009.

EDUCATION

A quarter of our teachers are very good. If you could make all the teachers as good as the top quarter, the US would soar to the top of that comparison. So can you find the way to capture what the really good teachers are doing? It's amazing to me that more has not been invested in looking at how does that good teacher calm that classroom? How does that good teacher keep the attention of all those kids? We need to measure what they do, and then have incentives for the other teachers to learn those things.

—*Newsweek*, 20 December 2010.

....

If I hadn't had great teachers during those years I wouldn't have learned how cool science and math are. In fact, I had a bad biology teacher and it's only as an adult that I've realized, hey, biology might be the most interesting science of all. But I stayed away from it.

—Black Enterprise, October 2011.

EDUCATION REFORM

Schools can have an extended day [so that] if a student is having trouble with math work, there would be a set of videos he or she could watch and exercises to try out that are set up and personalised. And the number of adults who need to be around is quite small because a lot of the instructional pace is being driven by technology.

—*Ebony*, October 2011.

We have two big theories about how we might ... change things. One is to help improve the quality of teaching [which] means really studying why some teachers are so much better than others. There is some magic stuff being done by the best teachers. And yet there is not really an effort to transfer those skills to other teachers. One of the ways to change that is through ... feedback. You get peers to come in and see what you're doing. If there is a digital camera in the classroom you can even review yourself.

—Black Enterprise, October 2011.

EFFECTIVE MEETINGS

When I go to a meeting, I keep specific objectives in mind. There isn't much small talk, especially if I'm with colleagues I know well. We discuss accounts we lost or where overhead is too high, and then we're done. Bang! There are always more challenges than there are hours, so why be wasteful?

—*New York Times* News Service/Syndicate,
19 February 1996.

....

We never waste a lot of time talking about what we're doing well. It just isn't our culture. Every meeting is about 'Sure, we won in seven of the categories, but what about that eighth category?'

—*Newsweek*, 1 December 1996.

EMPLOYEES

Take our twenty best people away, and I will tell you that Microsoft would become an unimportant company.

— *Masters of Enterprise*, 1999.

EMPLOYEES

Smart people anywhere in the company should have the power to drive an initiative.

— *Business @ The Speed of Thought*, 1999.

Microsoft's awareness that something very dramatic was going on around the Internet really came from an employee, so he became a change agent at Microsoft.

— *What the Best CEOs Know*, 2005.

ENCOURAGING PEOPLE TO GIVE TO CHARITY

I always say to people with a lot of money, 'Do you want a disease? We can give you this whole disease, or a whole region or a country. Whatever you want.' We heard again and again this recitation of places where all this great work had occurred and then it would just get stalled. There was just nobody to push it to the next level.

— *The New Yorker*, 24 October 2005.

ENERGY POLICY

We can say that we want energy that costs, say, a quarter of what coal electricity does and emits zero CO_2. But there are many paths to get there, each of which a realist would look at and say, 'Wow, there [are] a lot of difficult things along that path.' It is disappointing that some people have painted this problem as easy to solve. It's not easy, and it's bad for society if we think it is, because then funding for R&D doesn't happen.

— *Technology Review*, 1 September 2010.

...

If you're going for cuteness, the stuff in the home is the place to go. It's really kind of cool to have solar panels on your roof. But if you're really interested in the energy problem, it's [massive solar plants] in the desert.

— *Wired*, July 2011.

ENTREPRENEURS

Believe me, when somebody's in their entrepreneurial mode — being fanatical, inventing new things — the value they're adding to the world is phenomenal. If they invent new technologies, that is an amazing thing. And they don't even have to know how it's going to help people. But it will: in education, medical research, you name it.

— *Technology Review*, 1 September 2010.

The entrepreneurial mindset continues to thrive at Microsoft because one of our major goals is to reinvent ourselves — we have to make sure that we are the ones replacing our products instead of someone else.

— *Industry Week*, 20 November 1995.

ERADICATING DISEASE

When diseases affect both rich and poor countries, trickle-down will eventually work for the poorest, because the high cost of development is recovered in the rich world, and then as they go off patent, they're sold for marginal cost to the poor and everybody benefits.

— *Creative Capitalism*, 2008.

It may not be eradication, but making [AIDS] no longer something that is spreading in dramatic numbers like it is today and [ensuring that malaria is] something that children do not die from. The progress will be amazing, since so little has been done on these things.

— *Telegraph*, 1 February 2004.

ETHANOL

Despite often-heard claims to the contrary, ethanol has nothing to do with reducing CO_2; it's just a form of farm subsidy. If you're using first-class land for biofuels, then you're competing with the growing of food. And so you're actually spiking food prices by moving energy production into agriculture. For rich people, this is OK. For poor people, this is a real problem, because their food budget is an extremely high percentage of their income.

— *Wired*, July 2011.

FAILURE

I've always been hardcore about looking at what we did wrong. We're not known for reflecting back on the things that went well. We can be pretty brutal about the parts that don't do well.

—*Masters of Enterprise*, 1999.

FAMILY LIFE

My priority in life is my family. I always knew I'd get married and have children. You know, family life is all about [being] emotional and sharing things and doing things with each other.

—*20/20*, 30 JANUARY 1998.

I never took a day off in my twenties. Not one. And I'm still fanatical, but now I'm a little less fanatical. I play tennis, I play bridge, I spend time with my family. I drive myself around town in a normal Mercedes. I've had a Lexus. The family has a Porsche, which is a nice car that we sometimes take out. We have a minivan and that's what we use when it's the five of us. My eldest daughter rides horses, so we go to a lot of three-day shows. The kids are a big part of my schedule.

—MAIL ONLINE, 12 JUNE 2011.

When you choose to get married and have kids, if you're going to do it well, you are going to give up some of the fanaticism.

— *WIRED*, MAY 2010.

FASHION SENSE

There was one point in my life when my mother was trying to explain to me about what colour shirt to wear with what ties … And I think people listen to their mother's advice when it relates to fashion. It's not an area in which I claim to know more than she does … I don't look down at the colour I'm wearing during the day. So if it pleases other people that I know a little bit more about which shirt to pick with which tie, that's fine … I think I know a little bit about it now, but below average.

—*Playboy*, July 1994.

FAST FOOD

I eat at McDonald's more than most people, but that's because I don't cook … In terms of fast food and deep understanding of the culture of fast food, I'm your man.

—*Playboy*, July 1994.

(HIS) FATHER

… [M]y dad has set an example by what he does … whether it was at the university, speaking out on tough political issues, or going to war, or being a great lawyer … he's the one who really got the foundation going, encouraged me to give early, got us involved in some very key causes and helped us build what is now a strong group of people that I get to work with full-time. So my dad is somebody I aspire to live up to what he's done.

— *Charlie Rose Show*, 22 December 2008.

FEAR

Fear should guide you, but it should be latent. I have some latent fear. I consider failure on a regular basis.

—*Playboy*, July 1994.

FIGHTING HIV/AIDS

We need tools that will allow women to protect themselves. This is true whether the woman is a faithful married mother of small children, or a sex worker trying to scrape out a living in a slum. No matter where she lives, who she is, or what she does — a woman should never need her partner's permission to save her own life.

—KEYNOTE SPEECH, 16TH INTERNATIONAL AIDS CONFERENCE, 13 AUGUST 2006.

FIRST-WORLD COUNTRIES

Rich countries can afford to overpay for things. We can afford to overpay for medicine, we can overpay for energy, we can rig our food prices and overpay for cotton.

— *WIRED*, JULY 2011.

We will really have to screw things up for our absolute wealth not to increase.

— *THE WORLD IS FLAT*, 2005.

(HIS) FOUNDATION

The motto of the foundation is that every life has equal value. There are more people dying of malaria than any specific cancer. When you die of malaria aged three it's different from being in your seventies, when you might die of a heart attack or you might die of cancer. And the world is putting massive amounts into cancer, so my wealth would have had a meaningless impact on that.

—MAIL ONLINE, 12 JUNE 2011.

It's really drawn me in. And I find the same magic elements that made me love my work at Microsoft.

—*BUSINESSWEEK*, 12 FEBRUARY 2009.

I get to learn new things. But bringing top people together, taking risks, feeling like something very dramatic can come out of it — that's something that the previous work and the work now have in common.

—*BUSINESSWEEK*, 12 FEBRUARY 2009.

[One] way that running a foundation is not like running a business is that you don't have customers who beat you up when you get things wrong or competitors who work to take those customers away from you. You don't have a stock price that goes up and down to tell you how you're doing. This lack of a natural feedback loop means that we as a foundation have to be even more careful in picking our goals and being honest with ourselves when we are not achieving them.

—Bill & Melinda Gates Foundation, Annual Letter 2009.

We do family planning. We fund research on crops. Some people think that you shouldn't take science to help the poor people. This whole thing about which operating system somebody uses is a pretty silly thing versus issues involving starvation or death.

—*Newsweek*, 30 June 2008.

FUTURE OF TECHNOLOGY

I think short of the transporter, most things you see in science fiction are, in the next decade, the kinds of things you'll see. The virtual presence, the virtual worlds that both represent what's going on in the real world and represent whatever people are interested in. This movement in space as a way of interacting with the machine. I think the deep investments that have been made at the research level will pay off with these things in the next ten years.

—D5: All Things Digital conference, 30 May 2007.

GEEKS

Hey, if being a geek means you're willing to take a 400-page book on vaccines and where they work and where they don't, and you go off and study that and you use that to challenge people to learn more, then absolutely. I'm a geek. I plead guilty. Gladly.

—Mail Online, 12 June 2011.

If being a nerd means you're somebody who can enjoy exploring a computer for hours and hours late into the night, then the description fits me, and I don't think there's anything pejorative about it. But here's the real test: I've never used a pocket protector, so I can't really be a nerd, can I?

— *New York Times* News Service/Syndicate, 5 August 1996.

GETTING CAUGHT OFF GUARD

Sometimes we do get taken by surprise. For example, when the Internet came along, we had it as a fifth or sixth priority … But there came a point when we realised it was happening faster and was a much deeper phenomenon than had been recognized in our strategy.

— CNNMoney/*Fortune*, 20 July 1998.

GETTING IT RIGHT

In every product we ship, the team knows of features that I asked them to put in that they didn't get in. So you never ship a perfect software product. Thank goodness you don't, because then what would you do?

— *Newsweek*, 21 June 2008.

GIVING MONEY TO CHARITY

In giving money, you have to be as careful as you are in making money. You want to make sure it goes to good causes. And so, if you just spend it in an unthinking way, it can be gone in a second.

— *20/20*, 30 JANUARY 1998.

GIVING MONEY TO CHARITY

We do not measure ourselves at all by the amount given. We have taken on the top twenty killers, and for everything we do we look at the cost per life saved and real outcomes in terms of how things get improved. It's fun, and it is also an enormous responsibility … That is true for being a parent. Many of the most important things in life are like that. Why else would you want to get up in the morning?

— *The New Yorker*, 24 October 2005.

It's all the greater crime that something like malaria never got more attention. We gave a small grant at first, like thirty million dollars, and everybody said, 'Wow! That is the greatest increase in non-government spending in the history of malaria research!' And I thought, Oh, you are kidding.

— *The New Yorker*, 24 October 2005.

GIVING MONEY TO NON-AMERICAN CHARITIES

If you look and say where is the greatest inequity, you have to take a global view of that. I mean, America stands for a lot of things. It stands for the innovation that a capitalistic society can drive. It stands for political freedom. But it also stands for ending inequity.

—CNN, 5 October 2008.

GLOBAL HEALTH

Global health is our lifelong commitment. Until we reduce the burden on the poor so that there is no real gap between us and them, that will always be our priority. I am not so foolish as to say that will happen. But that's our goal.

— *The New Yorker*, 24 October 2005.

GLOBAL PROGRESS

The world is getting better, but it's not getting better fast enough, and it's not getting better for everyone.

— *Creative Capitalism*, 2008.

GOING WITH HIS GUT

Rationality only goes so far.

—*Creative Capitalism*, 2008.

GOOGLE

They have some of the same problems we had. They are hiring a lot of smart people. They have gotten into the lead position in search, which is incredibly profitable to be number one in that. They may get a little competition as time goes forward. But they are a great example of what can happen, you know, two young guys who got together, pursued an idea and created a success that's absolutely gigantic.

—CNBC Town Hall Event, Columbia University, 12 November 2009.

A great company.

—BBC News Online, 24 January 2004.

GOVERNMENT'S ANTITRUST CASE AGAINST MICROSOFT

What you have here is, basically, the US government saying our products are too capable.

—CNET, 27 January 1998.

The hard-core truth is that we've done nothing wrong.

—*Playboy*, July 1994.

There's no doubt that we wouldn't have a [Department of Justice] dispute here if some of our competitors hadn't decided that battling it out in the marketplace was — that their product wasn't going to do well enough on its own that way, that they were going to try and use the government to cripple us. And I use that word very carefully, because the idea of trying to tell us to ship products with features deleted, those are crippled products.

—Keynote speech, San Jose State, 27 January 1998.

When your own government sues you, it's not a pleasant experience. I wasn't sitting there going, 'ha, ha, ha, I'll do what I want.' I was thinking this is the worst thing that's ever happened to me.

—*ZD Net*, 28 January 1998.

HARVARD

Harvard was just a phenomenal experience for me. Academic life was fascinating. I used to sit in on lots of classes I hadn't even signed up for.

—COMMENCEMENT ADDRESS, HARVARD UNIVERSITY, 7 JUNE 2007.

....

There were very smart people to talk to. They fed you every day. [But] you didn't have to go to classes.

—*MICROSOFT REBOOTED*, 2004.

HIRING EMPLOYEES

Our hiring was always focused on people right out of school. We had a few key hires like Charles Simonyi who came in with experience. But most of our developers, we decided that we wanted them to come with clear minds, not polluted by some other approach, to learn the way that we liked to develop software, and to put the kind of energy into it that we thought was key.

—SMITHSONIAN INSTITUTION ORAL AND VIDEO HISTORIES, 2003.

We like people who have got an enthusiasm, for the product, technology, who really believe that it can do amazing things. We're very big on hiring smart people, so you'd better be comfortable working with other smart people, and kind of having the debate, and questioning that goes along with that.

—Keynote speech, San Jose State, 27 January 1998.

HIRING FOREIGN EMPLOYEES

Many people who look at offshoring are looking to save costs. [But] that's not the key thing. It's the quality, the innovation, how quickly we get things done. If you look at the pipeline, it's going to be a tougher and tougher situation for us to hire. You want to have some diversity, particularly in research where you can draw on the talent pool that's there. There's no doubt that if we had easy hiring here in the US, we would be doing more in the US.

— *Morning Edition*, 29 April 2005.

We [can] tap into the energy and talent of five times as many people as we did before.

— *The World is Flat*, 2005.

It's absolutely critical that we have an environment in which great minds from many countries can work together. We rely on skilled foreign workers for their math, science and creative abilities as well as their cultural knowledge, which helps when localising products for world markets.

—*New York Times* News Service/Syndicate,
20 December 1995.

HIS HOUSE

When you visit, you'll get an electronic PIN encoded with your preferences. As you wander toward any room, your favourite pictures will appear along with the music you like or a TV show or movie you're watching. The system will learn from your choices, and it will remember the music or pictures from your previous visits so you can choose to have them again or have similar but new ones.

—*Time*, 13 January 1997.

HOW HE DEFINES HIMSELF

I devote maybe 10 per cent to business thinking. Business isn't that complicated. I wouldn't want to put it on my business card. [I'm a] scientist. Unless I've been fooling myself. When I read about great scientists like, say, Crick and Watson and how they discovered DNA, I get a lot of pleasure. Stories of business success don't interest me in the same way. Say you added two years to my life and let me go to business school. I don't think I would have done a better job at Microsoft.

—*Playboy*, July 1994.

HOW HE'LL BE REMEMBERED

You know, who knows how history will think of me? You know, the person who played bridge with Warren Buffett, maybe. Or maybe not at all.

—CNN, 5 October 2008.

HOW HE'S SOFTENED OVER THE YEARS

In my twenties, I just worked.
Now I go home for dinner.

— *Wired*, May 2010.

HOW HE'S SOFTENED OVER THE YEARS

I don't think that IQ is as fungible as I used to. To succeed, you also have to know how to make choices and how to think more broadly.

— *Time*, 13 January 1997.

IBM

It's easy for people to forget how pervasive IBM's influence over this industry was. When you talk to people who've come into the industry recently there's no way you can get that into their heads, that was the environment.

— *Triumph of the Nerds*, June 1996.

The relationship between IBM and Microsoft was always a culture clash. IBMers were buttoned-up organisation men. Microsoftees were obsessive hackers. With the development of OS/2 the strains really began to show.

— *Triumph of the Nerds*, June 1996.

DEAL EMPLOYEES

If somebody is very smart and contributing a lot, then it is fun. If they don't match that kind of level of energy, then it is really not the right place for them. It is an exciting thing. It is still a little bit different.

—SMITHSONIAN INSTITUTION ORAL AND VIDEO HISTORIES, 2003.

Smart people ought to be able to figure anything out if they get enough facts.

—*SHOWSTOPPER!*, 1994.

IMMIGRATION POLICY

I think every country in the world should make it easier for people with high skills to come in.

I'm a big believer that as much as possible, and there are obviously political limitations, freedom of migration is a good thing.

—REUTERS, 21 MARCH 2007.

INTERNET

The beauty of the Internet is its openness. It cannot be controlled or dominated or cut off because it is simply a constantly changing series of linkages.

—CNNMoney, 3 March 1998.

INTRODUCING NEW PRODUCTS

Whenever you do a new piece of software you decide whether it is date driven or feature driven ... The key for Microsoft is that it is OK for us to be early [with the launch of new products]. We can afford to be early. What we do not want to do is be late.'

—*Telegraph*, 1 February 2004.

IPODS

I don't have an iPod. A phone is a nice portable device to have your music on. Maybe some other people will think so too in the future.

—*The Big Idea*, 8 May 2006.

IT EMPLOYEES

The money that companies spend on knowledge workers is a phenomenal amount. Whether those people do their jobs well is a huge part of whether the company is successful or not, so equipping them is not just a CIO thing. You've got to ask, 'Are these clerk-type jobs?' Because if they are, they are likely to go away. Or 'Are these thinking-type jobs?' In which case you should give the people pretty darn good tools and have the jobs be interesting enough that you can attract your share or better of the smart people to your company. That really is a business issue for the CEO.

—CNNMONEY/*FORTUNE*, 12 APRIL 1999.

IT INDUSTRY

Every year that we've existed, we've had the excitement that this is a fast-changing business. This wouldn't be a fun business if it wasn't always risky.

—*NEWSWEEK*, 30 JUNE 2008.

It's a fast-moving industry and no one has a guaranteed position ... I like our position better than others, but it's not in any sense guaranteed in any way.

—*INFOWORLD*, 21 NOVEMBER 1994.

(HIS) KIDS

[Jennifer, his three-year-old daughter] is a little redhead with brown eyes, the happiest person I've ever met. Everything she does is just so fascinating.

—*Newsweek*, 30 August 1999.

....

The more you force them by picking your choice, the more they will go away from it.

—Pomona College, 20 March 2011.

(HIS) KIDS PLAYING XBOX

Absolutely ... as opposed to sitting and passively watching TV, particularly as we bring in the social element. Now I wouldn't hold that up against, say, doing your homework or reading books. I think parents have to budget their kids' time, but interactive gaming fits in the mix, and it's getting a lot better.

—*Morning Edition*, 29 April 2005.

(A) KINDER AND GENTLER MICROSOFT

There is a huge responsibility to reach out, to be part of a broader dialogue; to reach out to Washington D.C., and be part of the spam dialogue; to reach out to Brussels and share what we see coming down there. So in terms of the company being kinder and gentler ... ever since we have been really successful, that's been very important. We get smarter about how to do it partly by making mistakes. We have the resources and the cleverness to look at those mistakes.

—*Microsoft Rebooted*, 2004.

LACK OF SUCCESS WITH WOMEN IN COLLEGE

Radcliffe was a great place to live. There were more women up there, and most of the guys were math–science types. That combination offered me the best odds, if you know what I mean. That's where I learned the sad lesson that improving your odds doesn't guarantee success.

—Commencement address, Harvard University, 7 June 2007.

LEAVING MICROSOFT

I've done the same thing for thirty-three years, in a sense ... It will be an adjustment for me. If I didn't have the Foundation — which is so exciting, and the work is complex — if I didn't have that, it would be tough for me, because I'm not a sit-on-the-beach type.

—*Seattle Post-Intelligencer*, 23 June 2008.

LEAVING MONEY TO HIS KIDS

But I don't think it would be beneficial to them to have huge amounts of wealth. I think that's very distortive in terms of how you think of what the impact you're going to have, how you measure yourself, how your friends think about you and how they do things with you. And it's also bad for society.

—CNN, 5 October 2008.

LEGACY

Legacy is a stupid thing! I don't want a legacy. If people look and see that childhood deaths dropped from nine million a year to four million because of our investment, then wow!

—Mail Online, 12 June 2011.

It will be a minuscule portion of my wealth. It will mean they have to find their own way. They will be given an unbelievable education and that will all be paid for. And certainly anything related to health issues we will take care of. But in terms of their income, they will have to pick a job they like and go to work. They are normal kids now. They do chores, they get pocket money.

—MAIL ONLINE, 12 JUNE 2011.

LINUX

It's easier for our software to compete with Linux when there's piracy than when there's not.

—CNNMONEY/*FORTUNE*, 17 JULY 2007.

LIVING A NORMAL LIFE

Some people ask me why I don't own a plane ... Why? Because you can get used to that kind of stuff, and I think that's bad. It takes you away from normal experiences in a way that is probably debilitating. So I control that kind of thing intentionally. It's one of those discipline things. If my discipline ever broke down it would confuse me, too. So I try to prevent that.

—*Playboy*, July 1994.

It's easy to get spoiled by things that alienate you from what's important. I wouldn't want to get used to being waited on or driven around. Living in a way that is unique would be strange.

—*Playboy*, July 1994.

LOVING HIS JOB

I wouldn't trade places with anyone, but the reason I like my job so much is that we have to constantly stay on top of those things.

—*Triumph of the Nerds*, June 1996.

LUCK

It is unusual to have so much luck in one life, I think. But it's been a major factor in what I have been able to do.

—CNBC Town Hall Event, Columbia University, 12 November 2009.

(THE) MACINTOSH

The Mac was a very, very important milestone. Not only because it established Apple as a key player in helping to find new ideas in the personal computer, but also because it ushered in graphical interface. [Back then], people didn't believe in graphical interface. And Apple bet their company on it, and that is why we got so involved in building applications for the Macintosh early on. We thought they were right. And we really bet our success on it as well. And today, all of the machines work that way because it is so much more natural. But this was pushing the limit.

—Smithsonian Institution Oral and Video Histories, 2003.

MAKING DECISIONS

Our decision process was very clear. There would be meetings I would be in and we would make those decisions. And so there was no confusion, there was no politicking, there was no overly long memo trying to explain something or posturing. That's how we would make those decisions ... You don't need a whole bunch of P&L owners or structure.

—*Microsoft Rebooted*, 2004.

Don't make the same decision twice. Spend time and thought to make a solid decision the first time so that you don't revisit the issue unnecessarily ... After all, why bother deciding an issue if it isn't really decided?

—*New York Times* News Service/Syndicate, 8 October 1997.

MAKING MISTAKES

There were a lot of missteps in the early days; because we got in early, we got to make more mistakes than other people.

—Smithsonian Institution Oral and Video Histories, 2003.

Many of our mistakes related to markets we didn't get into as early as we should have. The constraint was always the number of people we could hire, while still managing everything, and ensuring that we could meet all of our delivery commitments. We were always on the edge.

—FORBES.COM, 1 DECEMBER 1997.

MALARIA

The fact that malaria was eliminated in the United States and we don't need a malaria vaccine is a tiny bit of a tragedy because you don't have all of these brilliant minds at work to solve this problem.

— *CREATIVE CAPITALISM*, 2008.

It just blows my mind how little money has been spent on malaria research. What has prevented the rich world from attempting this? Do we really not care because it doesn't affect us? Human suffering as a result of malaria is incomparable. By many measures, it's easily the worst thing on the planet. I refuse to sit there and say, OK, next problem, this one doesn't bother me. It does bother me. And the only way for that to change is to stop malaria. So that is what we are going to have to do.

— *THE NEW YORKER*, 24 OCTOBER 2005.

MANAGERS

We're very big on managers who are very much in touch with doing hands-on work, who appreciate the work that people underneath them are doing, and retain the skill sets to jump in and do some of it themselves. So they can understand what is the load like, what's hard, how's that going on, and pitch in when there is something that's particularly tough. We're big into managers that believe in a lot of communication. It's awful when you get a group that's kind of drifted, and the morale has gone down, and you wonder, why didn't you find out early, you know, you should always know that as soon as possible. And so managers really have to be in touch with all of their people.

—Keynote speech, San Jose State, 27 January 1998.

MANAGING EMPLOYEES

People do play computer games at work, but they also doodle with pencils. Do you take away their pencils? That's not the way a modern workforce is managed. You've got to trust people.

—*New York Times* News Service/Syndicate,
4 November 1996.

MARRIAGE

[Finding a wife] certainly took me a lot of time.

—CNNMoney/*Fortune*, 17 May 1993.

MARRIAGE

Married life is a simpler life. Who I spend my time with is established in advance.

—*Playboy*, July 1994.

I knew not to get married until later because I was so obsessed with [the personal computer]. That's my life's work.

—D5: All Things Digital conference, 30 May 2007.

[My expectations] have been completely fulfilled. I have a much more balanced life.

—*Newsweek*, 30 August 1999.

Amazingly, [Melinda] made me feel like getting married. Now that is unusual! It's against all my past rational thinking on the topic.

—*Playboy*, July 1994.

Microsoft's competitors have been quoted as hoping married life ... will distract me from my work. After two years of marriage, that hasn't happened, and I don't think it will anytime soon.

— *Working Woman*, January 1996.

MEETING PRODUCT DEADLINES

If you take quality as a given, you are always going to have some uncertainty in the date.

— *InfoWorld*, 21 November 1994.

MEETINGS

I like question-and-answer sessions because they allow me to get a sense of what people are excited about and what they are upset about.

— *Industry Week*, 20 November 1995.

MICROSOFT CAMPUS

I was always thinking that the environment [where] we did product development should be a fun environment, a lot like a college campus. And this idea of using small teams means you want to give them all the tools, all the computers, an individual office, whatever it takes so that they feel like they can concentrate on their jobs and be very creative.

—Smithsonian Institution Oral and Video Histories, 2003.

MICROSOFT STOCK

The whole process looked like a pain, and an ongoing pain once you're public. People get confused because the stock price doesn't reflect your financial performance. And to have a stock trader call up the chief executive and ask him questions is uneconomic — the ball bearings shouldn't be asking the driver about the grease.

—CNNMoney/*Fortune*, 21 July 1986.

(THE) MICROSOFT WAY

The key for us [has] always been hiring very smart people. There is no way of getting around, that in terms of IQ, you've got to be very elitist in picking the people who deserve to write software. Ninety-five per cent of the people shouldn't write complex software. And using small teams helps a lot.

—Smithsonian Institution Oral and Video Histories, 2003.

Microsoft is designed to write great software. We are not designed to be good at other things. We only know how to hire, how to manage, and how to globalise software products. The key was to never view ourselves as a service company. We had to be a product company. But it was an approach that would probably not apply to any other business.

—Forbes.com, 1 December 1997.

The outside perception and inside perception of Microsoft are so different. The view of Microsoft inside Microsoft is always kind of an underdog thing.

—CNNMoney/*Fortune*, 2 October 1995.

We're always worried about keeping our pace — staying ahead. We know all our products will be obsolete two or three years from now and that it's a very competitive industry where everybody wants to replace things we've done, and yet we're trying to grow and bring in new ideas.

— *InfoWorld*, 21 November 1994.

MICROSOFT'S CORPORATE CULTURE

One of the great things about our culture is that we always operate knowing that projects we work on are key to the success and survival of the company. We've never had a culture where we say, 'Boy, we're in great shape,' because we know how dynamic the industry really is. We know we have to replace our products in a dramatic way. Or people will just keep using the current version of Windows or Office.

— *Newsweek*, 16 April 2000.

[There is] plenty of challenge, which is why it's good we're not a culture that looks back and has to waste a lot of time celebrating what we have done well.

— *Microsoft Rebooted*, 2004.

Size fundamentally works against excellence. Microsoft has long been an aggressive supporter of small, focused work groups. As the company has grown, we have continually worked to have an organisation within an organisation. Small teams can communicate effectively and aren't encumbered by a big structure slowing them down.

—*Industry Week*, 20 November 1995.

We come in to work every day knowing that we can destroy the company ... and that we better keep our wits about us, make the long-term investments in research that are going to make a big difference and really drive things forward.

—Keynote speech, San Jose State, 27 January 1998.

MICROSOFT'S CORPORATE STRUCTURE

There's no one path at Microsoft. We have a very flat organisation. Sometimes ideas flow down, sometimes they flow up, or horizontally. Usually, someone will get an idea or identify a problem and send email to someone else. This may kick off a SWAT team to deal with it. At some point, the decision gets made face to face or over email. On strategic decisions, it may go to a senior VP or to me. By and large, we empower people to make decisions themselves.

—*Information Outlook*, 1 May 1997.

MICROSOFT'S STRENGTHS

Well, hey, we can't do everything — we don't expect to do everything. [But] we do a lot and we have a longer time horizon than anyone else.

—*PC Magazine*, 23 June 2008.

We had ideas that the giants of the time missed. We're always thinking about what we have missed that could keep us on top.

—*USA Today*, 24 August 1995.

MONEY

I think your psyche about money is set by the time you're in your early twenties. At this point I'm clearly not by some definition 'middle class'. Hopefully my psyche hasn't been too warped in terms of the way I'll set my kids' allowance and the way I'll think about what they should be exposed to. It will be a lot like what my parents did.

—*Newsweek*, 30 AUGUST 1999.

(HIS) MOTHER

In no sense would I say, 'Oh, I'm making a sacrifice because it's something my mother told me I ought to do. I am doing something my mother told me I ought to do, but it's going to be a lot of fun. And I feel good about the impact as well.

—*Newsweek*, 30 June 2008.

MULTITASKING

Because there aren't enough hours in the day, it's temping to try to do two things at once. Right now I'm perfecting reading a newspaper and riding an exercise bike at the same time — a very practical form of multitasking.

—*New York Times* News Service/Syndicate,
25 September 1997.

(HIS) MUSICAL TASTE

... the twelve-year-old is always worried about the nine-year-old listening to songs with bad words. So he's like, 'No! Skip that one!' So I only know some Lady Gaga songs.

—Mail Online, 12 June 2011.

NUCLEAR POWER

The nuclear industry has this amazing [safety] record, even equipment from generations one and two. But nuclear mishaps tend to come in these big events — Chernobyl, Three Mile Island, and now Fukushima — so it's more visible ... The good news about nuclear is that there's hardly been any innovation in the past three decades, so the room to do things differently is quite dramatic ... we basically say no human should ever be required to do anything, because if you judge by Chernobyl and Fukushima, the human element is not on your side.

— *Wired*, July 2011.

OLDER IT EMPLOYEES

It just seems bizarre to me, the idea of a sixty-year-old man trying to make hard calls about where we invest in R&D and how the pieces fit together.

— *Telegraph*, 1 February 2004.

When I was young, I didn't know any old people. When we did the microprocessor revolution, there was nobody old, nobody. It's weird how old this industry has become.

— *Wired*, May 2010.

OVERPOPULATION

The world today has 6.8 billion people. That's headed up to about nine billion. Now, if we do a really great job on new vaccines, health care, reproductive health services, we could lower that [forecast] by, perhaps, 10 or 15 per cent, but there we see an increase of about 1.3 [per year].

—TED TALK, FEBRUARY 2010.

OVERVALUING TECH COMPANIES

Froth is mostly good. It means that there are high levels of investment, and therefore there's a heightened pace of innovation and a corresponding fear of being left behind. That's almost a fad-type effect, but in this world there's a real phenomenon behind it that's pulling people into it, and that's good.

—CNNMONEY/*FORTUNE*, 12 APRIL 1999.

PARENTHOOD

The nice thing about being a parent is it gives you a long-term perspective. You start thinking about, 'OK, you know, when my kids are my age, what will the United States be like?' I also think about my kids showing interest in different things — you know, I won't push them, but I'd love to have them be in some part of the sciences where they can make a contribution that really improves the world.

— *Morning Edition*, 29 April 2005.

(HIS) PARENTS

In my parents I saw a model where they were really always communicating, doing things together ... they were really kind of a team. I wanted some of that magic myself.

— *Newsweek*, 30 August 1999.

PARTNERSHIPS

We always thought the best thing to do is to try and combine IBM promoting the software with us doing the engineering. And so it was only when they broke off communication and decided to go their own way that we thought, OK, we're on our own, and that was definitely very, very scary.

— *Triumph of the Nerds*, June 1996.

Our business strategy from the beginning was quite different than all the computer companies that existed when we were started. We decided to focus just on doing the high-volume software, not to build hardware systems, not to do chips, just to do software … It was a strategy that required partners. I think the most successful partnership in the history of American business is the work we've done with Intel. When we started working with them, both companies were worth one-hundredth of what they're worth today. And so, working hand-in-hand in a nice, complementary way, you know, with a little bit of friction from time to time because we're both pretty strong-willed companies, we built two of the most successful enterprises of the era.

— Keynote speech, San Jose State, 27 January 1998.

I always knew I would have close business associates ... that we would stick together and grow together no matter what happened. I didn't know that because of some analysis. I just decided early on that was part of who I was.

— *TIME*, 13 JANUARY 1997.

(THE) PAST

I don't waste much time ruing the past. I made my decision, and the way to do it best is, once you make it, you just don't waver at all ... Being hard-core and forward looking about what you do is a necessary element of doing it well.

—*FORBES ASAP*, 28 FEBRUARY 1994.

PAUL ALLEN

We were true partners. We'd talk for hours every day. [Today] we like to talk about how the fantasies we had as kids actually came true.

— *TIME*, 13 JANUARY 1997.

Paul was my friend from the early days. And we are very close friends today and I'm sure we always will be. He is very idea-oriented. He and I would brainstorm about things. So even though I was running the business, it was a partnership. His role was very, very critical to so many of the transitions that we made. [But] there was always some strain because I was pushing people to work hard, including Paul.

—SMITHSONIAN INSTITUTION ORAL AND VIDEO HISTORIES, 2003.

(HIS) PERSONALITY

This is how I see the world, and it should make one thing clear: I am an optimist. But I am an impatient optimist.

—*CREATIVE CAPITALISM*, 2008.

PHARMACEUTICAL COMPANIES

This leads to the paradox, that because the disease is only in the poor countries, there is not much investment. For example, there is more money put into baldness drugs than are put into malaria. Now baldness is a terrible thing and rich men are afflicted, so that is why that priority is set.

—TED TALK, FEBRUARY 2010.

PHILANTHROPY

You know, in a lot of philanthropy, things don't go very well.

—*Reading with the Stars*, 2011.

You think in philanthropy that your dollars will just be marginal, because the really juicy obvious things will all have been taken. So you look at this stuff and we are, like, 'Wow!' When somebody is saying to you we can save many lives for hundreds of dollars each, the answer has to be no, no, no. That would already have been done. We go to events where people are raising money for various illnesses where lives are being treated as if they were worth many millions of dollars. And here we were learning that you can save even more lives for a few hundred each. We really did think it was too shocking to be true.

—*The New Yorker*, 24 October 2005.

PLAYING COMPUTER GAMES

I am not as good as some of the young kids ... I find even the basic level pretty challenging.

— *Telegraph*, 1 February 2004.

PLAYING BRIDGE

Warren [Buffett] is still somewhat better than I am. He plays a lot more than I do ... about twenty hours a week. I don't get anywhere near that. In three or four years I will be a lot better than I am today.

— *Telegraph*, 1 February 2004.

POLITICS

In the early days of the company I was very proud that we had no lobbyists ever, no PACs. I had to spend more time in capitals of other countries than our capital. What a testament that was to America. You could build a company with great success without involvement in political activities of any kind.

— *Microsoft Rebooted*, 2004.

POVERTY

The great advances in the world have often aggravated the inequities in the world. The least needy see the most improvement, and the most needy see the least — in particular, the billion people who live on less than a dollar a day.

— *Creative Capitalism*, 2008.

PRESERVING CORPORATE CULTURE

People can't come and talk to me every day. And so they have to look to their Business Unit Manager, which is how we have it set up. Certainly, we are trying to preserve all of that culture, and get the advantages of being a large company with a broad product line, with stability, worldwide presence, great support, and yet have the advantages that a small software company has.

—Smithsonian Institution Oral and Video Histories, 2003.

PROGRAMMING

The finest pieces of software are those where one individual has a complete sense of exactly how the program works. To have that, you have to really love the program and concentrate on keeping it simple, to an incredible degree.

—*Programmers at Work*, 1986.

Sometimes I envy people who still get to program. After I stopped programming for Microsoft, I used to say half-jokingly in meetings: 'Maybe I'll come in this weekend and write it myself.' I don't say that anymore but I think about it.

—*New York Times* News Service/Syndicate, 14 March 1995.

PROMOTING FROM WITHIN

The way our ladder works, you can keep getting promoted to new levels just by being better at creating the product. It's important to set examples. When something works out, you take the guys involved in that project and you make them heroes. You let everyone know that people should strive to be like them.

—*Success Magazine*, October 1988.

PUBLIC PERCEPTION

I don't have any particular goal for how I'm perceived. In writing [*The Road Ahead*], I'm sharing my thoughts, you know, my optimism and sort of the way I think about the business challenges and some of the changes. I've never written down how I want people to think about me.

—*The Washington Post*, 3 December 1995.

When somebody's successful, people leap to simple explanations that might make sense. So you get these myths. People love to have any little story. Yes, I'm intense. I'm energetic. I like to understand what our market position is. But then it gets turned into this — the ultracompetitor. It's somewhat dehumanising. I read that and say, I don't know that guy.

—*Newsweek*, 30 August 1999.

RAPID GROWTH

I got to the point where I couldn't look at all of the code, which I had done in the early years. At 100 people, I knew everybody. I even knew their licence plates when they came and went. I knew really what everyone was up to. By the time it got to 1000 that was no longer the case. I was hiring the managers and knew all of the managers, but there was a level of indirection. And, certainly, as you go up over 10,000 then there ... are some managers you don't know.

—SMITHSONIAN INSTITUTION ORAL AND VIDEO HISTORIES, 2003.

RECEIVING AN HONORARY DEGREE FROM HARVARD

I've been waiting more than thirty years to say this: 'Dad, I always told you I'd come back and get my degree.'

—COMMENCEMENT ADDRESS, HARVARD UNIVERSITY, 7 JUNE 2007.

I want to thank Harvard for this timely honour. I'll be changing my job next year ... and it will be nice to finally have a college degree on my resume.

—COMMENCEMENT ADDRESS, HARVARD UNIVERSITY, 7 JUNE 2007.

RELIGION

In terms of doing things I take a fairly scientific approach to why things happen and how they happen. I don't know if there's a god or not, but I think religious principles are quite valid.

— *Talking with David Frost*, 1995.

I was raised religiously. And my wife and I definitely believe in raising our kids religiously. I'm a big believer in religious values. As far as, you know, the deep questions about God, it's not something that I think I personally have the answers.

— *20/20*, 30 January 1998.

Just in terms of allocation of time resources, religion is not very efficient. There's a lot more I could be doing on a Sunday morning.

— *Time*, 13 January 1997.

REPLYING TO A SUGGESTION THAT HE'S MELLOWED IN RECENT YEARS

Bullshit.

—*Seattle Post-Intelligencer*, 23 June 2008.

RELINQUISHING CONTROL

We definitely needed to change. The last few years of trying to do both things [oversee product strategy and act as CEO] were pretty tough. [The transition] has worked out exactly the way I thought it would … I get more time on products than I've had for ages and ages. [And] there is a set of things that Steve [Ballmer] gets to worry about that I don't have to worry about.

—*Telegraph*, 1 February 2004.

RETIRING

If you say, 'Gosh, I won't leave when there's an interesting competitor,' then you'd have to die on the job.

—*Newsweek*, 21 June 2008.

RISK

A little blindness is necessary when you undertake a risk. You have to have a little suspension of disbelief where you say, 'Hey, we're going to do this unproven product. Let's do our best.'

— *The Costco Connection*, November 1997.

ROBOTICS

There are one hundred universities making contributions to robotics. And each one is saying that the other is doing it all wrong.

— *The World is Flat*, 2005.

ROTE-ORIENTED EDUCATION OF ASIAN STUDENTS

I have never met the guy who doesn't know how to multiply who created software. Who has the most creative video games in the world? Japan! I never met these [learning-by-] 'rote people'… Some of my best software developers are Japanese. You need to understand things in order to invent beyond them.

— *The World is Flat*, 2005.

RUNNING FOR POLITICAL OFFICE

I certainly will never be a politician ... for every reason. I wouldn't be elected, I'm better at what I'm doing. Whether it's time spent on Microsoft or the foundation ... I'm going to stick to what I know.

— *The Big Idea*, 8 May 2006.

SELF-CONFIDENCE

There become a few magic moments where you have to have confidence in yourself … When I dropped out of Harvard and said to my friends, 'Come work for me,' there was a certain kind of brass self-confidence in that. You have a few moments like that where trusting yourself and saying yes, this can come together — you have to seize on those because not many come along.

—CNBC Town Hall Event, Columbia University, 12 November 2009.

SHARING IDEAS

Whenever anybody else in the software industry wanted to know where we thought things were going, they'd come and talk to us. Because our vision, we shared; we didn't view that as some competitive edge. We just wanted to talk about it and get other people to share the same ideas so that they would help make it all come true.

—Smithsonian Institution Oral and Video Histories, 2003.

SILICON VALLEY

America has a lot to be proud of with this industry. [Silicon Valley] has benefitted immensely. The jobs have been created here, the wealth has been created here. You know, this is a story that everyone should feel good about [and that] the industry should feel good about.

—Keynote speech, San Jose State, 27 January 1998.

SOCIAL INEQUITY

Humanity's greatest advances are not in its discoveries, but in how those discoveries are applied to reduce inequity. Whether through democracy, strong public education, quality health care, or broad economic opportunity, reducing inequity is the highest human achievement.

—COMMENCEMENT ADDRESS, HARVARD UNIVERSITY, 7 JUNE 2007.

SOCIALLY CONSCIOUS CORPORATIONS

Profits are not always possible when business tries to serve the very poor. In such cases, there needs to be another market-based incentive — and that incentive is recognition. Recognition enhances a company's reputation and appeals to customers; above all, it attracts good people to the organisation.

— *CREATIVE CAPITALISM*, 2008.

SOFTWARE

If you look inside my brain, it's filled with software and, you know, the magic of software and the belief in software and, you know, that's not going to change.

—D5: ALL THINGS DIGITAL CONFERENCE 30 MAY 2007.

....

I'm very optimistic about software. I can't imagine why software is not the most overcrowded field in the world. What could be more interesting than working on these tough problems, and being able to have this kind of impact to build magic new devices? And, in fact, what I and my generation got to do these last thirty years really pales in comparison to what you'll be able to do in the next thirty years ahead.

—SPEECH, UNIVERSITY OF WASHINGTON, 25 APRIL 2008.

STEVE BALLMER

It's a phenomenal business partnership. I wouldn't enjoy my job like I do if it wasn't for how much fun Steve and I have brainstorming things. And within the company, everybody has understood that we work very closely together and have a very common view of where we want to go.

—*NEWSWEEK*, 23 JUNE 1997.

Steve was smart enough and personal enough, that even though he didn't have a technical background, the programmers accepted him. That was very rare. We didn't really believe non-programmers should manage programmers. But the developers accepted him early on because he was smart, he would sit and listen to them, understand the things that they really liked to do.

—Smithsonian Institution Oral and Video Histories, 2003.

Steve was supercritical, full of ideas, influencing everything we did — even technical things, how we would organise, what people we would pick. But I was the decision maker.

— *Microsoft Rebooted*, 2004.

Steve [Ballmer] had accepted that he wasn't going to get the visibility, the glory and the final decision on anything. And I was good at saying, Steve, do you want to say anything more [while making decisions]? But I had to make the final decision.

— *Working Together*, 2010.

The benefit of sparking off somebody who's got that kind of brilliance is that it not only makes business more fun, but it really leads to a lot of success.

—CNNMONEY/*FORTUNE*, 20 JULY 1998.

Steve is my best friend ... He was the opposite of me. I didn't go to classes much, wasn't involved in campus activities. Steve was involved in everything, knew everyone ... He got me to join the Fox Club, a men's club where you put on tuxedos, smoke cigars, drink too much, stand up on chairs and tell stories, play pool. Very old school.

—*FORBES*, 27 JANUARY 1997.

I have Steve look at my calendar. It's a conversation we have at least ten times a year: 'I'm feeling overloaded again. I wonder if I'm spending my time the right way?' And so Steve will get my calendar and flip through it and say, 'Did you really need to do this speech? Did you need to meet with these guys?'

—*NEWSWEEK*, 23 JUNE 1997.

STEVE JOBS

I'd give a lot to have Steve's taste.

—D5: ALL THINGS DIGITAL CONFERENCE, 30 MAY 2007.

In terms of an inspirational leader, Steve Jobs is really the best I've ever met. I mean, he can make people work, you know, more than they should. He's got to be careful, it's such a strong power, he can overuse it. You know, I always say to him, he's a first-class magician, and I can recognise him, because I'm kind of a second-class magician. It doesn't mean I can do what he does, but I can kind of tell, wow, that's powerful stuff. As far as I'm concerned, what he did … was just unbelievable. He drove that team to do something that was a fantastic contribution.

—KEYNOTE SPEECH, SAN JOSE STATE, 27 JANUARY 1998.

The world rarely sees someone who has had the profound impact Steve has had, the effects of which will be felt for many generations to come. For those of us lucky enough to get to work with him, it's been an insanely great honour. I will miss Steve immensely.

—ALL THINGS DIGITAL, 5 OCTOBER 2011.

He, of all the leaders in the industry that I have worked with, showed more inspiration and he saved the company.

—CNBC Town Hall Event, Columbia University, 12 November 2009.

STREAMLINING BUSINESS PROCESSES

We didn't need a lot of formal process because, believe me, it's better to have three guys who really know what's going on than to have all of the processes that allow twelve to all sort of think they are part of that decision process.

—*Microsoft Rebooted*, 2004.

SUCCESS

Success is a lousy teacher. It seduces smart people into thinking they can't lose.

— *The Road Ahead*, 1995.

SUCCESS

Smartness is an ability to absorb new facts. To walk into a situation, have something explained to you, and immediately say, 'Well, what about this?' To ask an insightful question. To absorb it in real time. A capacity to remember. To relate to domains that may not seem connected at first.

— *The Rich & How they Got that Way*, 2001.

We were in the right place at the right time. We got there first.

— *What the Best CEOs Know*, 2005.

We win because we hire the smartest people. We improve our products based on feedback, until they're the best. We have retreats each year where we think about where the world is heading.

— *Time*, 13 January 1997.

Our success has really been based on partnerships from the very beginning.

— *The Road Ahead*, 1995.

TAKING SUCCESS FOR GRANTED

No one's got a guaranteed position in the high technology business.

—*Triumph of the Nerds*, June 1996.

TAXING THE RICH

If you don't give it away, yes, I think some portion of it ought to be taxed, that there would be an estate tax. After all, the accretion of that fortune depended on the government's educational system, justice system. You know, it wasn't something where you just went off on your own and magically pulled some gold out of the ground.

—CNN, 5 October 2008.

TECHNOLOGICAL DEVELOPMENT

Just as movies entertain and move audiences, the creation and acceptance of technology has its own set of plot twists — often with uncertain or surprise endings.

—*Hollywood Reporter*, 5 September 2002.

With technology we've always got that people tend to overestimate what can change in a year or two, and they underestimate the cumulative effect of change that can take place in a ten- or fifteen-year period.

—SPEECH, UNIVERSITY OF WASHINGTON, 25 APRIL 2008.

TECHNOLOGICAL OBSOLESCENCE

There's not a single line of code here today that will have value in, say, four or five years' time. Today's operating systems will be obsolete in five years.

—*MASTERS OF ENTERPRISE*, 1999.

TECHNOLOGY AND EDUCATION

Technology is only lightly connected to the classroom experience today. The view is that it could be used in a new way ... You put these short lectures online for free and then you're actually going to that lecture part outside the classroom. And so you use the classroom time for problem solving if there is something you are confused about, or sophisticated ways of looking at the concept.

—BLACK ENTERPRISE, OCTOBER 2011.

TECHNOLOGY BOOMS AND BUSTS

This period in the late 1990s when people thought startups could do everything, people didn't care about research and the long-term effort required to do speech recognition, visual recognition. It got a little frustrating. All this capital was being thrown at those people, and they weren't really doing multi-product, long-term things, they were just kind of doing this one thing, but that was messing up the way that our work was looked at.

—*NEWSWEEK*, 21 JUNE 2008.

TEENAGE YEARS

The hard-core years, the most fanatical years, are thirteen to sixteen. By the time I was seventeen, my software mind had been shaped.

—*HACKERS*, 2010.

TELEVISION

I don't have any TVs with their over-the-air receivers connected in my house. But when I'm in a hotel room or other places that have a TV, then I turn it on and flip the channels just like everybody else. I was watching cartoons on Nickelodeon on Sunday, *Ren & Stimpy* and *Rugrats*. Cartoons have improved a lot since I was a kid. I'm not immune to the lures of television. I just try to stay away from it because I like to read.

—*Playboy*, July 1994.

THINKING

People must have time to think about things.

—*Advertising Age*, 23 September 1996.

VACATION

When I go on vacation, although I do long-term thinking about the company, I don't do email. Email is the key to me. For me in terms of a real break it is when you're not doing email. At Christmas and two other times a year, I will have a vacation where, unless there is some real problem, I stay off email. There also better be a beach and the kids and some other things.

—*Microsoft Rebooted*, 2004.

WARREN BUFFETT

He has this very refreshing, simple way of looking at things.

—*GUARDIAN*, 5 MAY 2006.

Warren Buffett is the closest thing I have to a role model because of the integrity and thoughtfulness and joy he brings to everything he does. I'm continuing to learn from my dad, I'm continuing to learn from Warren, and many times when I'm making decisions, I try and model how they'd approach a problem.

—*CHARLIE ROSE SHOW*, 22 DECEMBER 2008.

Warren and I love [listening] to questions and talking about our optimism.

—CNBC TOWN HALL EVENT, COLUMBIA UNIVERSITY, 12 NOVEMBER 2009.

I think Warren has had more effect on the way I think about my business and the way I think about running it than any business leader. He's got a way of thinking long term, a way of analysing the business fundamentals that the way he does it he makes it all seem so simple. Well, of course, you know, he's analysing in all these factors, and he's thinking way ahead of everybody else. But there's an immense value gotten out of that, as well as enjoy[ing] him as a friend. He's just an incredible person.

—KEYNOTE SPEECH, SAN JOSE STATE, 27 JANUARY 1998.

He loves to teach. He does it meeting with students. He does it in his annual newsletter. He does it when he's talking to me on the phone. It's a real gift that I admire incredibly.

—CNBC TOWN HALL EVENT, COLUMBIA UNIVERSITY, 12 NOVEMBER 2009.

WATCHING CHEMISTRY LECTURES

Everybody should watch chemistry lectures — they're far better than you think. Don Sadoway, MIT — best chemistry lessons everywhere. Unbelievable.

—*SEATTLE POST-INTELLIGENCER*, 23 JUNE 2008.

WEALTH

Ridiculous sums of money
can be confusing.

—*Playboy*, JULY 1994.

WEALTH

I wish I wasn't [wealthy] ... There's nothing good that comes out of that. You do get more visibility as a result of it.

— *Guardian*, 5 May 2006.

WHAT MAKES HIM MAD

Not much.

— *The Big Idea*, 8 May 2006.

(HIS) WIFE

The simplest thing to say about Melinda is that I fell deeply in love with her and decided to get married and have a family together.

— *20/20*, 30 January 1998.

WORK HABITS

I'm not big on to-do lists.

—CNNMoney, 7 April 2006.

WORKING WITH HIS WIFE

[Melinda] and I enjoy sharing ideas and talking about what we are learning. When one of us is being very optimistic, the other takes on the role of making sure we're thinking through all the tough issues.

— *Working Together*, 2010.

Melinda and I get very hands-on and involved in these things, and once we pick something, we like to see it through.

—*Reading with the Stars*, 2011.

WORLDVIEW

I believe in intensity.

— *Hackers*, 2010.

It's possible, you can never know, that the universe exists only for me. If so, it's sure going well for me, I must admit.

— *Time*, 13 January 1997.

I'm an optimist. I think this is a wonderful time to be alive. There have never been so many opportunities to do things that were impossible before.

— *The Road Ahead*, 1995.

MILESTONES

1955

BG born in Seattle to William H and Mary Maxwell Gates. (28 October.)

1967

Bill Gates III — nicknamed Trey because his father, Bill Gates Sr, customarily used the suffix 'II' after his name — begins attending the Lakeside School, a private college preparatory school where many children from Seattle's wealthy and elite families were enrolled, including Paul Allen.

1968

At age thirteen, BG writes his first computer program in BASIC on an old Teletype Model 33 terminal at school.

1970

BG starts a business with Paul Allen. Their main product is 'Traf-o-Data', a program to help keep tabs on traffic patterns.

1972

BG works as a congressional page in the United States House of Representatives over the summer.

1973

BG graduates from Lakeside in June after scoring 1590 out of 1600 points on the SAT. BG is accepted into the pre-law program at Harvard University.

He becomes friends with Steve Ballmer, who lives in the same dorm.

1974

BG takes a summer job with electronics firm Honeywell, joining Paul Allen, who had dropped out of college to work there.

1975

An article about the Altair 8800, manufactured by Micro Instrumentation and Telemetry Systems — MITS — appears in *Popular Electronics*, captivating BG. He and Paul Allen write BASIC software for the computer, and the manufacturer — based in Albuquerque — hires the pair.

BG leaves Harvard in his junior year and moves to Albuquerque with Allen; they christen their partnership Micro-Soft.

1976

BG and Allen officially register Microsoft — without the hyphen — as a business organisation.

Computer hobbyists had acquired copies of BASIC, which they used and passed along to others, without paying Microsoft. BG writes a scathing letter accusing the hobbyists of theft.

1977

Microsoft severs ties with MITS. BG writes and develops other computer languages, including FORTRAN, for various companies and contractors.

BG is arrested in Albuquerque for speeding.

1978

Microsoft opens its first international office, in Japan.

Company revenues hit US$1 million.

1979

Microsoft moves its offices to Bellevue, Washington. Twenty-five employees work full-time for the company, which generates US$2.5 million in revenue that year.

1980

Microsoft strikes a deal with IBM to provide the DOS operating system software for their line of personal computers, scheduled to be produced and sold the following year. BG retains the rights to MS-DOS, allowing Microsoft to license the operating system to other PC manufacturers.

Steve Ballmer joins Microsoft as personal assistant to BG.

1981

Microsoft officially becomes a corporation, naming BG as chairman and CEO. Steve Ballmer becomes executive vice-president of sales and support. BG receives 53 per cent of Microsoft, Allen gets 31 per cent and Ballmer has 8 per cent.

The IBM Personal Computer debuts. (August.)

Microsoft has 128 employees and annual revenues of US$16 million.

Steve Jobs of Apple Computer asks BG and Microsoft to develop software for their new computer, named the Macintosh.

1983

Instead of announcing a 'Man of the Year', *Time* names the personal computer as 'Machine of the Year'.

Paul Allen is diagnosed with Hodgkin's disease and leaves Microsoft.

1984

Apple Computer launches the Macintosh. (January.)

1985

The first incarnation of Windows launches, which many believe is similar to the Macintosh. (20 November.)

Annual revenue hits US$140 million; 910 employees work at Microsoft.

1986

Microsoft's first common stock is issued. With 45 per cent of the 24.7 million shares issued, BG earns US$234 million the first day of trading.

BG moves Microsoft's 1200 employees from Bellevue to new headquarters in Redmond, Washington.

1987

Forbes names BG a billionaire in its annual list of the 400 Richest People.

At thirty-one, BG becomes the youngest billionaire in history.

BG meets Melinda French, a Microsoft Product Manager, at a Microsoft event in New York City.

1988

Apple sues Microsoft, accusing BG and the company of designing Windows to mimic the Macintosh design too closely.

1989

BG launches Corbis, a digital archive of art and photography.

Microsoft introduces Microsoft Office, which incorporates several software programs, including Word and Excel.

1990

Microsoft launches Windows 3.0. As a result of its overwhelming popularity — more than 100,000 copies sell in just two weeks — annual sales at Microsoft reach US$1 billion for the year.

Microsoft had been developing an operating system with IBM called OS/2, but pulls out in order to concentrate on Windows.

The Federal Trade Commission starts looking into anticompetitive practices between Microsoft and IBM.

1992

BG hits the top of the *Forbes* 400 Richest People list, becoming the richest person in the United States, with US$6.3 billion in personal wealth.

1993

BG proposes marriage to Melinda French, who accepts.

The FTC decides to pass on the antitrust issue, instead referring it to the Department of Justice.

1994

BG marries Melinda French on in Lanai, Hawaii. (1 January.)

BG buys Leonard da Vinci's *Codex Leicester* for US$30.8 million at auction.

BG launches the William H Gates Foundation, officially marking the start of his philanthropic career.

Mary Gates, BG's mother, dies of breast cancer. (June.)

1995

Windows 95 launches; it incorporates the web browser Internet Explorer. (1 January.)

BG's first book is published. *The Road Ahead* hits number one on *The New York Times* bestseller list and stays there for almost two months.

His fortune pegged at US$12.9 billion, BG is named by *Forbes* as the richest man in the world.

Despite initially underestimating the Internet's potential, BG sends Microsoft executives a memo directing them to focus on developing software for the Internet.

1996

BG and Melinda's first daughter, Jennifer Katharine, is born. (26 April.)

Warren Buffett replaces BG as world's richest man as declared by *Forbes*. BG drops to second place.

Internet Explorer 3.0 launches.

Netscape, a company developing a browser, requests that the Justice Department look into Microsoft for bundling Internet Explorer with Windows.

1997

After seven years of construction, BG moves his family into a 66,000-square-foot house on Lake Washington in Medina. It's estimated that the house cost US$97 million to build.

1998

Microsoft launches Windows 98.

Steve Ballmer becomes president of Microsoft.

The US Department of Justice and twenty state's attorneys file an antitrust suit against Microsoft, accusing the company of participating in anticompetitive practices.

1999

BG and Melinda's son, Rory John, is born. (23 May.)

BG's second book, *Business @ the Speed of Thought*, is published in twenty-five languages.

2000

Microsoft launches two separate versions of Windows: 2000 and Me, short for Millennium Edition.

BG passes his title of Microsoft CEO to Steve Ballmer; Gates officially becomes known as Chief Software Architect.

The judge in the anti-trust trial orders Microsoft to become two companies: one for Windows and one for all other software. BG appeals the ruling.

BG and Melinda Gates launch the Bill & Melinda Gates Foundation, incorporating several other foundations, with an initial contribution of US$28 billion from personal funds.

Global annual revenues for Microsoft hit US$229 billion; the number of employees is almost 40,000.

2001

The judge's decision in the anti-trust trial is overturned. Microsoft and the Department of Justice reach an agreement that keeps the company intact.

Windows XP is introduced.

Microsoft launches the Xbox, a video game console.

2002

BG and Melinda's second daughter, Phoebe Adele, is born. (14 September.)

2004

BG becomes a board member at Berkshire Hathaway, friend Warren Buffett's investment business.

The European Commission launches an anti-trust investigation against Microsoft.

2005

Time names Bill and Melinda Gates and U2's Bono as its Persons of the Year because of their philanthropic work.

BG receives an honorary knighthood from Queen Elizabeth.

2006

Warren Buffett gives the bulk of his wealth, US$31 billion, to the Bill & Melinda Gates Foundation.

BG announces that he will step down from his full-time job at Microsoft in 2008.

BG receives the 2006 James C Morgan Global Humanitarian Award.

2007

BG receives an honorary doctor of law degree from Harvard; he gives the commencement speech at the ceremony.

Microsoft introduces Windows Vista and Office 2007.

2008

The European Union fines Microsoft $1.4 billion, the largest fine ever levied against a European business, claiming the company has not followed through on an earlier EU ruling, ordering the company to give specific software code to its competitors.

BG spends his last day at Microsoft. He stays on as chairman. (27 June.)

The number of Microsoft employees hits 90,000.

2009

Despite losing US$18 billion in net worth, BG usurps friend Warren Buffett as *Forbes'* number one billionaire in the world, retaining US$40 billion in personal wealth.

BG quits using Facebook because too many people wanted to friend him.

2010

BG attends the Sundance Film Festival to help promote *Waiting for Superman*, a documentary that he helped to fund on America's failing education system.

BG rejoins Facebook, and signs up for Twitter as well.

2011

BG loses the top spot on *Forbes'* richest person in the world list because he's given away so much money, but is still second on the list, with US$53 billion; Buffett is third for the year. BG is still the wealthiest American.

Rumours swirl late in the year that BG would return to Microsoft. No dice, he says; he likes his foundation work too much.

CITATIONS

ACQUIRING OTHER COMPANIES

'Bill Gates Keynote Speech: A Conversation with Bill Gates', San Jose State, San Jose, CA, 27 January 1998. http://web.archive.org/web/20100909091356/http://www.microsoft.com/presspass/exec/billg/speeches/1998/sanjose.aspx

ADDICTION TO TECHNOLOGY

Susan Lammers, *Programmers at Work*, 'Bill Gates – 1986' (Redmond, Washington: Microsoft Press, 1986). http://www.programmersatwork.wordpress.com/bill-gates-1986/

AFRICAN-AMERICAN EDUCATIONAL DISPARITY

Kevin Chappell, 'One-on-One with Bill Gates', *Ebony*, October 2011.

AIR TRAVEL

Bill Gates, column, *New York Times* News Service/Syndicate, 29 August 1995.

AMERICA

'Warren Buffett & Bill Gates: Keeping America Great', CNBC Town Hall Event transcript, Columbia University, 12 November 2009.
http://www.cnbc.com/id/33901003/CNBC_TRANSCRIPT_Warren_Buffett_Bill_Gates_Keeping_America_Great

AMERICAN UNIVERSITIES

Thomas L Friedman, *The World is Flat: A Brief History of the Twenty-first Century* (New York: Farrar, Straus and Giroux, 2005).

ANALYSING OTHER COMPANIES

Bill Gates, 'Watch Time, Competition, Systems in Quest for Success', *New York Times* News Service/Syndicate, 19 February 1996.

ANDY GROVE

'Bill Gates Keynote Speech: A Conversation with Bill Gates', San Jose State, San Jose, CA, 27 January 1998.
http://web.archive.org/web/20100909091356/http://www.microsoft.com/presspass/exec/billg/speeches/1998/sanjose.aspx

(HIS) ANTISOCIAL TENDENCIES

Commencement address, Harvard University, Cambridge, MA, 7 June 2007.
http://www.harvardmagazine.com/2007/07/harvard-2007-commencement-address

ANTI-VACCINE PROPONENTS

Danielle Dellorto, 'Bill Gates: Vaccine–Autism Link "An Absolute Lie"', CNN, 4 February 2011.
http://www.cnn.com/2011/HEALTH/02/03/gupta.gates.vaccines.world.health/index.html

APPLE

'Bill Gates Praising Apple Computers', speech, YouTube, 1984.
http://www.youtube.com/watch?v=Uau0aIbrzkQzz

BAD NEWS

'Bill Gates Keynote Speech: A Conversation with Bill Gates', San Jose State, San Jose, CA, 27 January 1998.
http://web.archive.org/web/20100909091356/http://www.microsoft.com/presspass/exec/billg/speeches/1998/sanjose.aspx

BEING CEO

'The View from the Very Top', *Newsweek*, 16 April 2000.
http://www.thedailybeast.com/newsweek/2000/04/16/the-view-from-the-very-top.html

BEING IN CHARGE

David Allison, 'Bill Gates Interview', Smithsonian Institution Oral and Video Histories, 2003.
http://americanhistory.si.edu/collections/comphist/gates.htm

BEING THE FACE OF MICROSOFT

Mark Whitaker, 'How we Did it', *Newsweek*, 23 June 1997.
http://www.thedailybeast.com/newsweek/1997/06/22/how-we-did-it.html
Steven Levy, 'Gates, Face to Face', *Newsweek*, 1 December 1996.
http://www.thedailybeast.com/newsweek/1996/12/01/gates-face-to-face.html

Kit R. Roane, 'Gates to Give Up Microsoft Reins', *U.S. News & World Report*, 16 June 2006.
http://www.usnews.com/usnews/biztech/articles/060616/16gates.htm

BONO

Bill Gates, Speech on Creative Capitalism, 2008 World Economic Forum, 24 January 2008.
http://www.gatesfoundation.org/speeches-commentary/Pages/bill-gates-2008-world-economic-forum-creative-capitalism.aspx
Amanda Ripley and Amanda Bower, 'From Riches to Rags', *Time*, 26 December 2005.
http://www.time.com/time/magazine/article/0,9171,1142276,00.html

BREAKTHROUGHS

Steven Levy, 'He's Still Having Fun', *Newsweek*, 24 November 2003.
http://www.thedailybeast.com/newsweek/2003/11/23/he-s-still-having-fun.html

BUSINESS COMPUTING

Bill Gates, Speech on Digital Nervous System, Enterprise Perspective, New York, 24 March 1999.

BUSINESS CUSTOMERS

Michael Miller, 'The Bill Gates Exit Interview', *PC Magazine*, 23 June 2008.
http://www.pcmag.com/article2/0,2817,2320850,00.asp
Bill Gates, *Business @ the Speed of Thought* (New York: Grand Central Publishing, 1999).

BUSINESS STANDARDS

Bill Gates, 'Next-Generation Software', Rosen Research Personal Computer Forum Proceedings, May 1981.

CAPITALISM

Cynthia Crossen, *The Rich & How they Got that Way* (Boston: Nicholas Brealey Publishing, 2001).
'Warren Buffett & Bill Gates: Keeping America Great', CNBC Town Hall Event transcript, Columbia University, 12 November 2009.
http://www.cnbc.com/id/33901003/CNBC_TRANSCRIPT_Warren_Buffett_Bill_Gates_Keeping_America_Great

CAREER

Becky Anderson, 'Interview with Bill Gates', *Connect the World*, CNN, 20 July 2010.
http://transcripts.cnn.com/TRANSCRIPTS/1007/20/ctw.01.html
Bill Gates, 'Riches not What Spurred this Dreamer', *New York Times* News Service/Syndicate, 27 October 1996.

CEDING POWER TO BALLMER

Robert Guth, 'Gates–Ballmer Clash Shaped Microsoft's Coming Handover', *The Wall Street Journal*, 5 June 2008.

CHALLENGES

'The View from the Very Top', *Newsweek*, 16 April 2000.
http://www.thedailybeast.com/newsweek/2000/04/16/the-view-from-the-very-top.html

CHANGE

David Allison, 'Bill Gates Interview', Smithsonian Institution Oral and Video Histories, 2003.
http://americanhistory.si.edu/collections/comphist/gates.htm
Commencement address, Harvard University, Cambridge, MA, 7 June 2007.
http://www.harvardmagazine.com/2007/07/harvard-2007-commencement-address

CHILDHOOD

Michael Miller, 'The Bill Gates Exit Interview', *PC Magazine*, 23 June 2008.
http://www.pcmag.com/article2/0,2817,2320850,00.asp
James Wallace, *Hard Drive: Bill Gates and the Making of the Microsoft Empire* (New York: John Wiley & Sons, 1992).

CHINA

Corey Grice and Sandeep Junnarkar, 'Gates, Buffett a Bit Bearish', CNET News, 2 July 1998.
http://news.cnet.com/2100-1023-212942.html
'Warren Buffett & Bill Gates: Keeping America Great', CNBC Town Hall Event transcript, Columbia University, 12 November 2009.
http://www.cnbc.com/id/33901003/CNBC_TRANSCRIPT_Warren_Buffett_Bill_Gates_Keeping_America_Great
Thomas L Friedman, *The World is Flat: A Brief History of the Twenty-first Century* (New York: Farrar, Straus and Giroux, 2005).
Steve Inskeep, 'Gates: U.S. Losing Advantage in Innovation Race', *Morning Edition*, NPR, 29 April 2005.
http://www.npr.org/templates/story/story.php?storyId=4624316
Walter Isaacson, 'In Search of the Real Bill Gates', *Time*, 13 January 1997.
http://www.time.com/time/magazine/article/0,9171,1120657,00.html
Thomas L Friedman, *The World is Flat: A Brief History of the Twenty-first Century* (New York: Farrar, Straus and Giroux, 2005).

CLIMATE CHANGE

Chris Anderson, 'Q&A: Bill Gates on the World's Energy Crisis', *Wired*, July 2011.
www.wired.com/magazine/2011/06/mf_qagates/all/1

CLONING

Barbara Walters, 'The Mind of Bill Gates', *20/20*, ABC, 30 January 1998.

CLOUD COMPUTING

Michael Miller, 'The Bill Gates Exit Interview', *PC Magazine*, 23 June 2008.
http://www.pcmag.com/article2/0,2817,2320850,00.asp

COLLEGE EDUCATION

Bill Gates, column, *New York Times* News Service/Syndicate, 13 May 1996.

COMPETITION

'Apple v. Microsoft', *Telegraph*, 11 February 2010.
http://www.telegraph.co.uk/technology/7213348/Apple-v-Microsoft-What-Steve-Jobs-and-Bill-Gates-really-think-of-each-other.html
Fareed Zakaria, *Global Public Square*, CNN, 5 October 2008.
http://transcripts.cnn.com/TRANSCRIPTS/0810/05/fzgps.01.html
Bill Gates, 'Watch Time, Competition, Systems in Quest for Success', *New York Times* News Service/Syndicate, 19 February 1996.
HW Brands, *Masters of Enterprise* (New York: Free Press, 1999).
G Pascal Zachary, *Showstopper! The Breakneck Race to Create Windows NT and the Next Generation at Microsoft* (New York: Free Press, 1994).

COMPUTERS VS. PEOPLE

Bill Gates, *The Road Ahead* (New York: Viking, 1995).

CONCEPT OF TIME

Steven Levy, 'Microsoft after Gates. (And Bill after Microsoft)', *Newsweek*, 30 June 2008.
http://www.thedailybeast.com/newsweek/2008/06/21/microsoft-after-gates-and-bill-after-microsoft.html

CONTINUING TO WORK AFTER BECOMING A BILLIONAIRE

Walter Isaacson, 'In Search of the Real Bill Gates', *Time*, 13 January 1997.
http://www.time.com/time/magazine/article/0,9171,1120657,00.html

COOPERATION

Michael D Eisner and Aaron R Cohen, *Working Together: Why Great Partnerships Succeed* (New York: HarperBusiness, 2010).
Jason Pontin, 'Q&A: Bill Gates', *Technology Review,* 1 September 2010.
http://www.technologyreview.com/energy/26112

CORPORATE ANTI-DISCRIMINATION POLICY

Steve Inskeep, 'Gay Rights Law Divided Microsoft, Gates Says', *Morning Edition*, NPR, 28 April 2005.
http://www.npr.org/templates/story/story.php?storyId=4622804

CORPORATE SOCIAL RESPONSIBILITY

Michael Kinsley, *Creative Capitalism* (New York: Simon and Schuster 2008).

CORPORATE STRATEGY

Louise Kehoe and Hugo Dixon, 'The FT Interview', *Financial Times*, 10 June 1996.

CORPORATE WORKING ENVIRONMENT

Brent Schlender, 'E-Business According to Gates', CNNMoney/*Fortune*, 12 April 1999.
http://money.cnn.com/magazines/fortune/fortune_archive/1999/04/12/258104/index.htm

CREATIVITY

Bill Gates, *New York Times* News Service/Syndicate, 9 October 1996.

Sarah Blaskovich, 'Lessons from a New-Product Wizard', *Success Magazine*, October 1988.
http://www.successmagazine.com/article/print?articleId=347

CRITICISING EMPLOYEES

David Rensin, 'The Bill Gates Interview', *Playboy*, July 1994.

CRITICS

HW Brands, *Masters of Enterprise* (New York: Free Press, 1999).
Steven Levy, 'Behind the Gates Myth', *Newsweek*, 30 August 1999.
http://www.thedailybeast.com/newsweek/1999/08/29/behind-the-gates-myth.html
Barbara Walters, 'The Mind of Bill Gates', *20/20*, ABC, 30 January 1998.
Walter Isaacson, 'In Search of the Real Bill Gates', *Time*, 13 January 1997.
http://www.time.com/time/magazine/article/0,9171,1120657,00.html
Steven Levy, 'Microsoft after Gates. (And Bill after Microsoft)', *Newsweek*, 30 June 2008.
http://www.thedailybeast.com/newsweek/2008/06/21/microsoft-after-gates-and-bill-after-microsoft.html

DECIDING WHICH PROJECTS TO FUND

'Warren Buffett & Bill Gates: Keeping America Great', CNBC Town Hall Event transcript, Columbia University, 12 November 2009.
http://www.cnbc.com/id/33901003/CNBC_TRANSCRIPT_Warren_Buffett_Bill_Gates_Keeping_America_Great
Commencement address, Harvard University, Cambridge, MA, 7 June 2007.
http://www.harvardmagazine.com/2007/07/harvard-2007-commencement-address

DELEGATING

Robert Slater, *Microsoft Rebooted: How Bill Gates and Steve Ballmer Reinvented Their Company* (New York: Portfolio, 2004).

DETERMINATION

James Wallace, *Hard Drive: Bill Gates and the Making of the Microsoft Empire* (New York: John Wiley & Sons, 1992).

DROPPING OUT OF HARVARD

Robert Cringely, *Triumph of the Nerds*, PBS, June 1996.
http://www.pbs.org/nerds/part1.html

EARLY COMPETITORS

David Allison, 'Bill Gates Interview', Smithsonian Institution Oral and Video Histories, 2003.
http://americanhistory.si.edu/collections/comphist/gates.htm

EARLY COMPUTERS

Jeffrey A. Krames, *What The Best CEOs Know* (New York: McGraw-Hill, 2005).

EARLY DAYS

Robert Cringely, *Triumph of the Nerds*, PBS, June 1996.
http://www.pbs.org/nerds/part1.html
Brent Schlender and Henry Goldblatt, 'Bill Gates & Paul Allen Talk', CNNMoney/*Fortune*, 2 October 1995.
http://money.cnn.com/magazines/fortune/fortune_archive/1995/10/02/206528/index.htm
HW Brands, *Masters of Enterprise* (New York: Free Press, 1999).
Steven Levy, 'A Big Birthday for Bill & Co.', *Newsweek*, 17 September 2000.
http://www.thedailybeast.com/newsweek/2000/09/17/a-big-birthday-for-bill-amp-co.html
James Wallace, *Hard Drive: Bill Gates and the Making of the Microsoft*

Empire (New York: John Wiley & Sons, 1992).
Brent Schlender and Henry Goldblatt, 'Bill Gates & Paul Allen Talk', CNNMoney/*Fortune*, 2 October 1995.
http://money.cnn.com/magazines/fortune/fortune_archive/1995/10/02/206528/index.htm

E-BOOKS

Caroline Graham, 'This Is Not the Way I'd Imagined Bill Gates', Mail Online, 12 June 2011.
http://www.dailymail.co.uk/home/moslive/article-2001697/Microsofts-Bill-Gates-A-rare-remarkable-interview-worlds-second-richest-man.html

ECONOMIC CRISIS

'Warren Buffett & Bill Gates: Keeping America Great', CNBC Town Hall Event transcript, Columbia University, 12 November 2009.
http://www.cnbc.com/id/33901003/CNBC_TRANSCRIPT_Warren_Buffett_Bill_Gates_Keeping_America_Great

EDUCATION

Daniel Lyons, 'Bill Gates and Randi Weingarten', *Newsweek*, 20 December 2010.
http://www.thedailybeast.com/newsweek/2010/12/20/gates-and-weingarten-fixing-our-nation-s-schools.html
Alan Hughes, 'Can Bill Gates Save Our Schools?', Black Enterprise, October 2011.
http://m.blackenterprise.com/p.p?m=b&a=rp&id=409116963&postId=409116963&postUserId=2609744

EDUCATION REFORM

Kevin Chappell, 'One-on-One with Bill Gates', *Ebony*, October 2011.
Alan Hughes, 'Can Bill Gates Save Our Schools?', Black Enterprise, October 2011.

http://m.blackenterprise.com/p.p?m=b&a=rp&id=409116963&postId=409116963&postUserId=2609744

EFFECTIVE MEETINGS

Bill Gates, 'Watch Time, Competition, Systems in Quest for Success', *New York Times* News Service/Syndicate, 19 February 1996.

Steven Levy, 'Gates, Face to Face', *Newsweek*, 1 December 1996. http://www.thedailybeast.com/newsweek/1996/12/01/gates-face-to-face.html

EMPLOYEES

HW Brands, *Masters of Enterprise* (New York: Free Press, 1999).

Bill Gates, *Business @ the Speed of Thought* (New York: Grand Central Publishing, 1999).

Jeffrey A Krames, *What The Best CEOs Know* (New York: McGraw-Hill, 2005).

ENCOURAGING PEOPLE TO GIVE TO CHARITY

Michael Specter, 'What Money Can Buy', *The New Yorker*, 24 October 2005.

ENERGY POLICY

Jason Pontin, 'Q&A: Bill Gates', *Technology Review*, 1 September 2010.

http://www.technologyreview.com/energy/26112

Chris Anderson, 'Q&A: Bill Gates on the World's Energy Crisis', *Wired*, July 2011.

www.wired.com/magazine/2011/06/mf_qagates/all/1

ENTREPRENEURS

Jason Pontin, 'Q&A: Bill Gates', *Technology Review*, 1 September 2010.

http://www.technologyreview.com/energy/26112

George Taninecz, 'Gates Wins Respect', *Industry Week*, 20 November 1995.

ERADICATING DISEASE

Michael Kinsley, *Creative Capitalism* (New York: Simon and Schuster, 2008).
Richard Fletcher, 'Gates' New Window on the World', *Telegraph,* 1 February 2004.
http://www.telegraph.co.uk/finance/2875628/Gates-new-window-on-the-world.html

ETHANOL

Chris Anderson, 'Q&A: Bill Gates on the World's Energy Crisis', *Wired,* July 2011.
www.wired.com/magazine/2011/06/mf_qagates/all/1

FAILURE

HW Brands, *Masters of Enterprise* (New York: Free Press, 1999).

FAMILY LIFE

Barbara Walters, 'The Mind of Bill Gates', *20/20,* ABC, 30 January 1998.
Caroline Graham, 'This Is Not the Way I'd Imagined Bill Gates', Mail Online, 12 June 2011.
http://www.dailymail.co.uk/home/moslive/article-2001697/Microsofts-Bill-Gates-A-rare-remarkable-interview-worlds-second-richest-man.html
Steven Levy, 'Geek Power: Steven Levy Revisits Tech Titans, Hackers, Idealists', *Wired,* May 2010.
http://www.wired.com/magazine/2010/04/ff_hackers/

FASHION SENSE

David Rensin, 'The Bill Gates Interview', *Playboy,* July 1994.

FAST FOOD

David Rensin, 'The Bill Gates Interview', *Playboy,* July 1994.

(HIS) FATHER

'An Hour with Bill Gates,' *Charlie Rose Show*, 22 December 2008.
http://www.charlierose.com/download/transcript/10576

FEAR

David Rensin, 'The Bill Gates Interview', *Playboy*, July 1994.

FIGHTING HIV/AIDS

Bill and Melinda Gates, 'We Need to Put the Power of HIV Prevention in the Hands of Women', 16th International AIDS Conference, PR Newswire Europe, 13 August 2006.
http://www.prnewswire.co.uk/cgi/news/release?id=177031

FIRST-WORLD COUNTRIES

Chris Anderson, 'Q&A: Bill Gates on the World's Energy Crisis', *Wired*, July 2011.
www.wired.com/magazine/2011/06/mf_qagates/all/1

Thomas L Friedman, *The World is Flat: A Brief History of the Twenty-first Century* (New York: Farrar, Straus and Giroux, 2005).

(HIS) FOUNDATION

Caroline Graham, 'This Is Not the Way I'd Imagined Bill Gates', Mail Online, 12 June 2011.
http://www.dailymail.co.uk/home/moslive/article-2001697/Microsofts-Bill-Gates-A-rare-remarkable-interview-worlds-second-richest-man.html

Maria Bartiromo, 'Melinda and Bill Gates on Making a Difference', *BusinessWeek*, 12 February 2009.
http://www.businessweek.com/magazine/content/09_07/b4119021540910.htm

Bill Gates, 'The Role of Foundations', Bill & Melinda Gates Foundation, Annual Letter 2009.
http://www.gatesfoundation.org/annual-letter/Pages/2009-role-of-foundations.aspx

Steven Levy, 'Microsoft after Gates. (And Bill after Microsoft)', *Newsweek*, 30 June 2008.
http://www.thedailybeast.com/newsweek/2008/06/21/microsoft-after-gates-and-bill-after-microsoft.html

FUTURE OF TECHNOLOGY

Kara Swisher and Walt Mossberg, 'Bill Gates & Steve Jobs Interview', D5: All Things Digital conference, Carlsbad, CA, 30 May 2007.
http://allthingsd.com/20070531/d5-gates-jobs-transcript/

GEEKS

Caroline Graham, 'This Is Not the Way I'd Imagined Bill Gates', Mail Online, 12 June 2011.
http://www.dailymail.co.uk/home/moslive/article-2001697/Microsofts-Bill-Gates-A-rare-remarkable-interview-worlds-second-richest-man.html
Bill Gates, column, *New York Times* News Service/Syndicate 5 August 1996.

GETTING CAUGHT OFF GUARD

Brent Schlender, 'The Bill & Warren Show', CNNMoney/*Fortune*, 20 July 1998.
http://money.cnn.com/magazines/fortune/fortune_archive/1998/07/20/245683/index.htm

GETTING IT RIGHT

Steve Levy, "There's No Year That I Didn't Love My Job", *Newsweek*, 21 June 2008.
http://www.thedailybeast.com/newsweek/2008/06/21/there-s-no-year-that-i-didn-t-love-my-job.html

GIVING MONEY TO CHARITY

Michael Specter, 'What Money Can Buy', *The New Yorker*, 24 October 2005.

Barbara Walters, 'The Mind of Bill Gates', *20/20,* ABC, 30 January 1998.

Michael Specter, 'What Money Can Buy', *The New Yorker,* 24 October 2005.

GIVING MONEY TO NON-AMERICAN CHARITIES

Fareed Zakaria, *Global Public Square*, CNN, 5 October 2008.
http://transcripts.cnn.com/TRANSCRIPTS/0810/05/fzgps.01.html

GLOBAL HEALTH

Michael Specter, 'What Money Can Buy', *The New Yorker,* 24 October 2005.

GLOBAL PROGRESS

Michael Kinsley, *Creative Capitalism* (New York: Simon and Schuster, 2008).

GOING WITH HIS GUT

Michael Kinsley, *Creative Capitalism* (New York: Simon and Schuster, 2008).

GOOGLE

'Warren Buffett & Bill Gates: Keeping America Great', CNBC Town Hall Event transcript, Columbia University, 12 November 2009.
http://www.cnbc.com/id/33901003/CNBC_TRANSCRIPT_Warren_Buffett_Bill_Gates_Keeping_America_Great

Tim Weber, 'Gates Forecasts Victory over Spam', BBC News Online, 24 January 2004.
http://news.bbc.co.uk/2/hi/business/3426367.stm

GOVERNMENT'S ANTITRUST CASE AGAINST MICROSOFT

Christopher Barr, 'Gates Lashes out at Press', CNET, 27 January 1998.
http://www.news.cnet.com/2100-1001-207548.html&olr.dt
David Rensin, 'The Bill Gates Interview', *Playboy*, July 1994.
'Bill Gates Keynote Speech: A Conversation with Bill Gates', San Jose State, San Jose, CA, 27 January 1998.
http://web.archive.org/web/20100909091356/http://www microsoft.com/presspass/exec/billg/speeches/1998/sanjose. aspx
Lisa Bowman, 'Gates Gives Critics an "F"', *ZD Net*, 28 January 1998.
http://www.zdnet.com/news/gates-gives-critics-an-f/98361

HARVARD

Commencement address, Harvard University, Cambridge, MA, 7 June 2007.
http://www.harvardmagazine.com/2007/07/harvard-2007-commencement-address
Robert Slater, *Microsoft Rebooted: How Bill Gates and Steve Ballmer Reinvented Their Company* (New York: Portfolio, 2004).

HIRING EMPLOYEES

David Allison, 'Bill Gates Interview', Smithsonian Institution Oral and Video Histories, 2003.
http://americanhistory.si.edu/collections/comphist/gates.htm
'Bill Gates Keynote Speech: A Conversation with Bill Gates', San Jose State, San Jose, CA, 27 January 1998.
http://web.archive.org/web/20100909091356/http://www. microsoft.com/presspass/exec/billg/speeches/1998/sanjose. aspx

HIRING FOREIGN EMPLOYEES

Steve Inskeep, 'Gates: U.S. Losing Advantage in Innovation Race', *Morning Edition*, NPR, 29 April 2005.
http://www.npr.org/templates/story/story.php?storyId=4624316
Thomas L Friedman, *The World is Flat: A Brief History of the Twenty-first Century* (New York: Farrar, Straus and Giroux, 2005).
Bill Gates, 'Immigration Bill May Push Research out of the U.S.', *New York Times* News Service/Syndicate, 20 December 1995.

HIS HOUSE

Walter Isaacson, 'In Search of the Real Bill Gates', *Time*, 13 January 1997.
http://www.time.com/time/magazine/article/0,9171,1120657,00.html

HOW HE DEFINES HIMSELF

David Rensin, 'The Bill Gates Interview', *Playboy*, July 1994.

HOW HE'LL BE REMEMBERED

Fareed Zakaria, *Global Public Square*, CNN, 5 October 2008.
http://transcripts.cnn.com/TRANSCRIPTS/0810/05/fzgps.01.html

HOW HE'S SOFTENED OVER THE YEARS

Walter Isaacson, 'In Search of the Real Bill Gates', *Time*, 13 January 1997.
http://www.time.com/time/magazine/article/0,9171,1120657,00.html
Steven Levy, 'Geek Power: Steven Levy Revisits Tech Titans, Hackers, Idealists', *Wired*, May 2010.
http://www.wired.com/magazine/2010/04/ff_hackers/

IBM

Robert Cringely, *Triumph of the Nerds*, PBS, June 1996.
http://www.pbs.org/nerds/part1.html

IDEAL EMPLOYEES

David Allison, 'Bill Gates Interview', Smithsonian Institution Oral and Video Histories, 2003.
http://americanhistory.si.edu/collections/comphist/gates.htm
G Pascal Zachary, *Showstopper! The Breakneck Race to Create Windows NT and the Next Generation at Microsoft* (New York: Free Press, 1994).

IMMIGRATION POLICY

'Bill Gates Backs Immigration Reform on Mexico Trip', Reuters, 21 March 2007.

INTERNET

'Gates Stands Tough', CNNMoney, 3 March 1998.
http://www.money.cnn.com/1998/03/03/technology/gates/

INTRODUCING NEW PRODUCTS

Richard Fletcher, 'Gates' New Window on the World', *Telegraph,* 1 February 2004.
http://www.telegraph.co.uk/finance/2875628/Gates-new-window-on-the-world.html

IPODS

Donny Deutsch, *The Big Idea,* CNBC, 8 May 2006.
http://adage.com/article/news/highlights-ms-summit/109042/

IT EMPLOYEES

Brent Schlender, 'E-Business According to Gates', CNNMoney/*Fortune,* 12 April 1999.
http://money.cnn.com/magazines/fortune/fortune_archive/1999/04/12/258104/index.htm

IT INDUSTRY

Steven Levy, 'Microsoft after Gates. (And Bill after Microsoft)', *Newsweek,* 30 June 2008.

http://www.thedailybeast.com/newsweek/2008/06/21/microsoft-after-gates-and-bill-after-microsoft.html
Jai Singh and Doug Barney, 'Gates Unguarded', *InfoWorld*, 21 November 1994.

(HIS) KIDS

Steven Levy, 'Behind the Gates Myth', *Newsweek*, 30 August 1999.
http://www.thedailybeast.com/newsweek/1999/08/29/behind-the-gates-myth.html
Marissa Acierto, 'Conversation with Bill Gates', Pomona College, 20 March 2011.

(HIS) KIDS PLAYING XBOX

Steve Inskeep, 'Gates: U.S. Losing Advantage in Innovation Race', *Morning Edition*, NPR, 29 April 2005.
http://www.npr.org/templates/story/story.php?storyId=4624316

(A) KINDER AND GENTLER MICROSOFT

Robert Slater, *Microsoft Rebooted: How Bill Gates and Steve Ballmer Reinvented Their Company* (New York: Portfolio, 2004).

LACK OF SUCCESS WITH WOMEN IN COLLEGE

Commencement address, Harvard University, Cambridge, MA, 7 June 2007.
http://www.harvardmagazine.com/2007/07/harvard-2007-commencement-address

LEAVING MICROSOFT

Todd Bishop and Tom Paulson, 'Gates Talks about Letting Go', *Seattle Post-Intelligencer*, 23 June 2008.
http://www.seattlepi.com/business/article/Q-A-Gates-talks-about-letting-go-the-future-and-1277371.php

LEAVING MONEY TO HIS KIDS

Fareed Zakaria, *Global Public Square*, CNN, 5 October 2008. http://transcripts.cnn.com/TRANSCRIPTS/0810/05/fzgps.01.html

Caroline Graham, 'This Is Not the Way I'd Imagined Bill Gates', Mail Online, 12 June 2011. http://www.dailymail.co.uk/home/moslive/article-2001697/Microsofts-Bill-Gates-A-rare-remarkable-interview-worlds-second-richest-man.html

LEGACY

Caroline Graham, 'This Is Not the Way I'd Imagined Bill Gates', Mail Online, 12 June 2011. http://www.dailymail.co.uk/home/moslive/article-2001697/Microsofts-Bill-Gates-A-rare-remarkable-interview-worlds-second-richest-man.html

LINUX

David Kirkpatrick, 'How Microsoft Conquered China', CNNMoney/*Fortune*, 17 July 2007. http://money.cnn.com/magazines/fortune/fortune_archive/2007/07/23/100134488/

LIVING A NORMAL LIFE

David Rensin, 'The Bill Gates Interview', *Playboy*, July 1994.

LOVING HIS JOB

Robert Cringely, *Triumph of the Nerds*, PBS, June 1996. http://www.pbs.org/nerds/part1.html

LUCK

'Warren Buffett & Bill Gates: Keeping America Great', CNBC Town Hall Event transcript, Columbia University, 12 November 2009.

http://www.cnbc.com/id/33901003/CNBC_TRANSCRIPT_Warren_Buffett_Bill_Gates_Keeping_America_Great

(THE) MACINTOSH

David Allison, 'Bill Gates Interview', Smithsonian Institution Oral and Video Histories, 2005.
http://americanhistory.si.edu/collections/comphist/gates.htm

MAKING DECISIONS

Robert Slater, *Microsoft Rebooted: How Bill Gates and Steve Ballmer Reinvented Their Company* (New York: Portfolio, 2004).
Bill Gates, 'What Makes a Good Manager', *New York Times* News Service/Syndicate, 8 October 1997.

MAKING MISTAKES

David Allison, 'Bill Gates Interview', Smithsonian Institution Oral and Video Histories, 2003.
http://americanhistory.si.edu/collections/comphist/gates.htm
Bill Gates, 'Watching His Windows', Forbes.com, 1 December 1997.
http://www.forbes.com/asap/1997/1201/142.html

MALARIA

Michael Kinsley, *Creative Capitalism* (New York: Simon and Schuster, 2008).
Michael Specter, 'What Money Can Buy', *The New Yorker,* 24 October 2005.

MANAGERS

'Bill Gates Keynote Speech: A Conversation with Bill Gates', San Jose State, San Jose, CA, 27 January 1998.
http://web.archive.org/web/20100909091356/http://www.microsoft.com/presspass/exec/billg/speeches/1998/sanjose.aspx

MANAGING EMPLOYEES

Bill Gates, 'The Network Computer as the PC's Evil Twin', *New York Times* News Service/Syndicate, 4 November 1996.

MARRIAGE

David Rensin, 'The Bill Gates Interview', *Playboy*, July 1994.
Kara Swisher and Walt Mossberg, 'Bill Gates & Steve Jobs Interview', D5: All Things Digital conference, Carlsbad, CA, 30 May 2007.
http://allthingsd.com/20070531/d5-gates-jobs-transcript/
Steven Levy, 'Behind the Gates Myth', *Newsweek*, 30 August 1999.
http://www.thedailybeast.com/newsweek/1999/08/29/behind-the-gates-myth.html
David Rensin, 'The Bill Gates Interview', *Playboy*, July 1994.
'Now Hear This', CNNMoney/*Fortune*, 17 May 1993.
http://money.cnn.com/magazines/fortune/fortune_archive/1993/05/17/77870/index.htm
Lynn Povich, 'On Line with Bill Gates', *Working Woman*, January 1996.

MEETING PRODUCT DEADLINES

Jai Singh and Doug Barney, 'Gates Unguarded', *InfoWorld*, 21 November 1994.

MEETINGS

George Taninecz, 'Gates Wins Respect', *Industry Week*, 20 November 1995.

MICROSOFT CAMPUS

David Allison, 'Bill Gates Interview', Smithsonian Institution Oral and Video Histories, 2003.
http://americanhistory.si.edu/collections/comphist/gates.htm

MICROSOFT STOCK

Bro Uttal and David Kirkpatrick, 'Inside the Deal that Made Bill Gates $350,000,000', CNNMoney/*Fortune*, 21 July 1986.
http://money.cnn.com/magazines/fortune/fortune_archive/1986/07/21/67877/index.htm

(THE) MICROSOFT WAY

David Allison, 'Bill Gates Interview', Smithsonian Institution Oral and Video Histories, 2003.
http://americanhistory.si.edu/collections/comphist/gates.htm
Bill Gates, 'Watching His Windows', Forbes.com, 1 December 1997.
http://www.forbes.com/asap/1997/1201/142.html
Brent Schlender and Henry Goldblatt, 'Bill Gates & Paul Allen Talk', CNNMoney/*Fortune*, 2 October 1995.
http://money.cnn.com/magazines/fortune/fortune_archive/1995/10/02/206528/index.htm
Jai Singh and Doug Barney, 'Gates Unguarded', *InfoWorld*, 21 November 1994.

MICROSOFT'S CORPORATE CULTURE

'The View from the Very Top', *Newsweek*, 16 April 2000.
http://www.thedailybeast.com/newsweek/2000/04/16/the-view-from-the-very-top.html
Robert Slater, *Microsoft Rebooted: How Bill Gates and Steve Ballmer Reinvented Their Company* (New York: Portfolio, 2004).
George Taninecz, 'Gates Wins Respect', *Industry Week*, 20 November 1995.
'Bill Gates Keynote Speech: A Conversation with Bill Gates', San Jose State, San Jose, CA, 27 January 1998.
http://web.archive.org/web/20100909091356/http://www.microsoft.com/presspass/exec/billg/speeches/1998/sanjose.aspx

MICROSOFT'S CORPORATE STRUCTURE

'A Conversation with Bill Gates', *Information Outlook*, 1 May 1997.

MICROSOFT'S STRENGTHS

Michael Miller, 'The Bill Gates Exit Interview', *PC Magazine*, 23 June 2008.
http://www.pcmag.com/article2/0,2817,2320850,00.asp
James Kim, 'Networking: Online Service Will Be Key', *USA Today*, 24 August 1995.

MONEY

Steven Levy, 'Behind the Gates Myth', *Newsweek*, 30 August 1999.
http://www.thedailybeast.com/newsweek/1999/08/29/behind-the-gates-myth.html

(HIS) MOTHER

Steven Levy, 'Microsoft after Gates. (And Bill after Microsoft)', *Newsweek*, 30 June 2008.
http://www.thedailybeast.com/newsweek/2008/06/21/microsoft-after-gates-and-bill-after-microsoft.html

MULTITASKING

Bill Gates, column, *New York Times* News Service/Syndicate, 25 September 1997.

(HIS) MUSICAL TASTE

Caroline Graham, 'This Is Not the Way I'd Imagined Bill Gates', Mail Online, 12 June 2011.
http://www.dailymail.co.uk/home/moslive/article-2001697/Microsofts-Bill-Gates-A-rare-remarkable-interview-worlds-second-richest-man.html

NUCLEAR POWER

Chris Anderson, 'Q&A: Bill Gates on the World's Energy Crisis', *Wired*, July 2011.
www.wired.com/magazine/2011/06/mf_qagates/all/1

OLDER IT EMPLOYEES

Richard Fletcher, 'Gates' New Window on the World', *Telegraph,* 1 February 2004.
http://www.telegraph.co.uk/finance/2875628/Gates-new-window-on-the-world.html

Steven Levy, 'Geek Power: Steven Levy Revisits Tech Titans, Hackers, Idealists', *Wired*, May 2010.
http://www.wired.com/magazine/2010/04/ff_hackers/

OVERPOPULATION

'Bill Gates on Energy: Innovating to Zero!' TED Talk, February 2010.
http://www.ted.com/talks/bill_gates.html

OVERVALUING TECH COMPANIES

Brent Schlender, 'E-Business According to Gates', CNNMoney/*Fortune*, 12 April 1999.
http://money.cnn.com/magazines/fortune/fortune_archive/1999/04/12/258104/index.htm

PARENTHOOD

Steve Inskeep, 'Gates: U.S. Losing Advantage in Innovation Race', *Morning Edition,* NPR, 29 April 2005.
http://www.npr.org/templates/story/story.php?storyId=4624316

(HIS) PARENTS

Steven Levy, 'Behind the Gates Myth', *Newsweek,* 30 August 1999.
http://www.thedailybeast.com/newsweek/1999/08/29/behind-the-gates-myth.html

PARTNERSHIPS

Robert Cringely, *Triumph of the Nerds*, PBS, June 1996.
http://www.pbs.org/nerds/part1.html

'Bill Gates Keynote Speech: A Conversation with Bill Gates', San Jose State, San Jose, CA, 27 January 1998.
http://web.archive.org/web/20100909091356/http://www.microsoft.com/presspass/exec/billg/speeches/1998/sanjose.aspx

Walter Isaacson, 'In Search of the Real Bill Gates', *Time*, 13 January 1997.
http://www.time.com/time/magazine/article/0,9171,1120657,00.html

(THE) PAST

Rich Karlgaard, 'On the Road with Bill Gates', *Forbes ASAP*, 28 February 1994.

PAUL ALLEN

Walter Isaacson, 'In Search of the Real Bill Gates', *Time*, 13 January 1997.
http://www.time.com/time/magazine/article/0,9171,1120657,00.html

David Allison, 'Bill Gates Interview', Smithsonian Institution Oral and Video Histories, 2003.
http://americanhistory.si.edu/collections/comphist/gates.htm

(HIS) PERSONALITY

Michael Kinsley, *Creative Capitalism* (New York: Simon and Schuster, 2008).

PHARMACEUTICAL COMPANIES

'Bill Gates on Energy: Innovating to Zero!' TED Talk, February 2010.
http://www.youtube.com/watch?v=ppDWD3VwxVg

PHILANTHROPY

Leonard Kniffel, *Reading with the Stars: A Celebration of Books and Libraries* (New York: Skyhorse Publishing, 2011).
Michael Specter, 'What Money Can Buy', *The New Yorker*, 24 October 2005.

PLAYING BRIDGE

Richard Fletcher, 'Gates' New Window on the World', *Telegraph*, 1 February 2004.
http://www.telegraph.co.uk/finance/2875628/Gates-new-window-on-the-world.html

PLAYING COMPUTER GAMES

Richard Fletcher, 'Gates' New Window on the World', *Telegraph*, 1 February 2004.
http://www.telegraph.co.uk/finance/2875628/Gates-new-window-on-the-world.html

POLITICS

Robert Slater, *Microsoft Rebooted: How Bill Gates and Steve Ballmer Reinvented Their Company* (New York: Portfolio, 2004).

POVERTY

Michael Kinsley, *Creative Capitalism* (New York: Simon and Schuster, 2008).

PRESERVING CORPORATE CULTURE

David Allison, 'Bill Gates Interview', Smithsonian Institution Oral and Video Histories, 2003.
http://americanhistory.si.edu/collections/comphist/gates.htm

PROGRAMMING

Susan Lammers, *Programmers at Work*, 'Bill Gates – 1986' (Redmond, Washington: Microsoft Press, 1986).
http://www.programmersatwork.wordpress.com/bill-gates-1986

Bill Gates, column, *New York Times* News Service/Syndicate, 14 March 1995.

PROMOTING FROM WITHIN

Sarah Blaskovich, 'Lessons from a New-Product Wizard', *Success Magazine*, October 1988.
http://www.successmagazine.com/article/print?articleId=347

PUBLIC PERCEPTION

Elizabeth Corcoran, 'Microsoft's Man', *The Washington Post*, 3 December 1995.
Steven Levy, 'Behind the Gates Myth', *Newsweek*, 30 August 1999.
http://www.thedailybeast.com/newsweek/1999/08/29/behind-the-gates-myth.html

RAPID GROWTH

David Allison, 'Bill Gates Interview', Smithsonian Institution Oral and Video Histories, 2003.
http://americanhistory.si.edu/collections/comphist/gates.htm

RECEIVING AN HONORARY DEGREE FROM HARVARD

Commencement address, Harvard University, Cambridge, MA, 7 June 2007.
http://www.harvardmagazine.com/2007/07/harvard-2007-commencement-address

RELIGION

David Frost, *Talking with David Frost: Bill Gates*, PBS Video 1995.
Barbara Walters, 'The Mind of Bill Gates', *20/20*, ABC, 30 January 1998.
Walter Isaacson, 'In Search of the Real Bill Gates', *Time*, 13 January 1997.
http://www.time.com/time/magazine/article/0,9171,1120657,00.html

RELINQUISHING CONTROL

Richard Fletcher, 'Gates' New Window on the World', *Telegraph,* 1 February 2004.
http://www.telegraph.co.uk/finance/2875628/Gates-new-window-on-the-world.html

REPLYING TO A SUGGESTION THAT HE'S MELLOWED IN RECENT YEARS

Todd Bishop and Tom Paulson, 'Gates Talks about Letting Go', *Seattle Post-Intelligencer,* 23 June 2008.
http://www.seattlepi.com/business/article/Q-A-Gates-talks-about-letting-go-the-future-and-1277371.php

RETIRING

Steve Levy, "There's No Year That I Didn't Love My Job", *Newsweek,* 21 June 2008.
http://www.thedailybeast.com/newsweek/2008/06/21/there-s-no-year-that-i-didn-t-love-my-job.html

RISK

'Technology', *The Costco Connection,* November 1997.

ROBOTICS

Thomas L Friedman, *The World is Flat: A Brief History of the Twenty-first Century* (New York: Farrar, Straus and Giroux, 2005).

ROTE-ORIENTED EDUCATION OF ASIAN STUDENTS

Thomas L Friedman, *The World is Flat: A Brief History of the Twenty-first Century* (New York: Farrar, Straus and Giroux, 2005).

RUNNING FOR POLITICAL OFFICE

Donny Deutsch, *The Big Idea,* CNBC, 8 May 2006.
http://adage.com/article/news/highlights-ms-summit/109042/

SELF-CONFIDENCE

'Warren Buffett & Bill Gates: Keeping America Great', CNBC Town Hall Event transcript, Columbia University 12 November 2009.
http://www.cnbc.com/id/33901003/CNBC_TRANSCRIPT_Warren_Buffett_Bill_Gates_Keeping_America_Great

SHARING IDEAS

David Allison, 'Bill Gates Interview', Smithsonian Institution Oral and Video Histories, 2003.
http://americanhistory.si.edu/collections/comphist/gates.htm

SILICON VALLEY

'Bill Gates Keynote Speech: A Conversation with Bill Gates', San Jose State, San Jose, CA, 27 January 1998.
http://web.archive.org/web/20100909091356/http://www.microsoft.com/presspass/exec/billg/speeches/1998/sanjose.aspx

SOCIAL INEQUITY

Commencement address, Harvard University, Cambridge, MA, 7 June 2007.
http://www.harvardmagazine.com/2007/07/harvard-2007-commencement-address

SOCIALLY CONSCIOUS CORPORATIONS

Michael Kinsley, *Creative Capitalism* (New York: Simon and Schuster, 2008).

SOFTWARE

Kara Swisher and Walt Mossberg, 'Bill Gates & Steve Jobs Interview', D5: All Things Digital conference, Carlsbad, CA, 30 May 2007.

http://allthingsd.com/20070531/d5-gates-jobs-transcript
Bill Gates, speech, College Tour 2008, University of Washington, Seattle, 25 April 2008.
http://www.microsoft.com/presspass/exec/billg/speeches/2008/04-25uw.mspx

STEVE BALLMER

Mark Whitaker, 'How we Did it', *Newsweek*, 23 June 1997.
http://www.thedailybeast.com/newsweek/1997/06/22/how-we-did-it.html
David Allison, 'Bill Gates Interview', Smithsonian Institution Oral and Video Histories, 2003.
http://americanhistory.si.edu/collections/comphist/gates.htm
Robert Slater, *Microsoft Rebooted: How Bill Gates and Steve Ballmer Reinvented Their Company* (New York: Portfolio, 2004).
Michael D Eisner and Aaron R Cohen, *Working Together: Why Great Partnerships Succeed* (New York: HarperBusiness, 2010).
Brent Schlender, 'The Bill & Warren Show', CNNMoney/*Fortune*, 20 July 1998.
http://money.cnn.com/magazines/fortune/fortune_archive/1998/07/20/245683/index.htm
Jeffrey Young, 'The George S Patton of Software', *Forbes*, 27 January 1997.
http://www.forbes.com/forbes/1997/0127/5902086a.html
Mark Whitaker, 'How we Did it', *Newsweek*, 23 June 1997.
http://www.thedailybeast.com/newsweek/1997/06/22/how-we-did-it.html

STEVE JOBS

Kara Swisher and Walt Mossberg, 'Bill Gates & Steve Jobs Interview', D5: All Things Digital conference, Carlsbad, CA, 30 May 2007.
http://allthingsd.com/20070531/d5-gates-jobs-transcript/
'Bill Gates Keynote Speech: A Conversation with Bill Gates', San Jose State, San Jose, CA, 27 January 1998.
http://web.archive.org/web/20100909091356/http://www.

microsoft.com/presspass/exec/billg/speeches/1998/sanjose.aspx
Ina Fried, 'Bill Gates: I Will Miss Steve Immensely', All Things Digital, 5 October 2011.
http://allthingsd.com/20111005/bill-gates-i-will-miss-steve-iImmensely
'Warren Buffett & Bill Gates: Keeping America Great', CNBC Town Hall Event transcript, Columbia University, 12 November 2009.
http://www.cnbc.com/id/33901003/CNBC_TRANSCRIPT_Warren_Buffett_Bill_Gates_Keeping_America_Great

STREAMLINING BUSINESS PROCESSES

Robert Slater, *Microsoft Rebooted: How Bill Gates and Steve Ballmer Reinvented Their Company* (New York: Portfolio, 2004).

SUCCESS

Bill Gates, *The Road Ahead* (New York: Viking, 1995).
Cynthia Crossen, *The Rich & How they Got that Way* (Boston: Nicholas Brealey Publishing, 2001).
Jeffrey A Krames, *What The Best CEOs Know* (New York: McGraw-Hill, 2005).
Walter Isaacson, 'In Search of the Real Bill Gates', *Time* 13 January 1997.
http://www.time.com/time/magazine/article/0,9171,1120657,00.html
Bill Gates, *The Road Ahead* (New York: Viking, 1995).

TAKING SUCCESS FOR GRANTED

Robert Cringely, *Triumph of the Nerds*, PBS, June 1996.
http://www.pbs.org/nerds/part1.html

TAXING THE RICH

Fareed Zakaria, *Global Public Square*, CNN, 5 October 2008.
http://transcripts.cnn.com/TRANSCRIPTS/0810/05/fzgps.01.html

TECHNOLOGICAL DEVELOPMENT

Chris Marlowe, 'Out of the Mouth of Gates', *Hollywood Reporter*, 5 September 2002.
http://www.homemediamagazine.com/news/from-the-hollywood-reporter-out-mouth-gates-3690

Bill Gates, speech, College Tour 2008, University of Washington, Seattle, 25 April 2008.
http://www.microsoft.com/presspass/exec/billg/speeches/2008/04-25uw.mspx

TECHNOLOGICAL OBSOLESCENCE

HW Brands, *Masters of Enterprise* (New York: Free Press, 1999).

TECHNOLOGY AND EDUCATION

Alan Hughes, 'Can Bill Gates Save Our Schools?', Black Enterprise, October 2011.
http://m.blackenterprise.com/p.p?m=b&a=rp&id=409116963&postId=409116963&postUserId=2509744

TECHNOLOGY BOOMS AND BUSTS

Steve Levy, "There's No Year that I Didn't Love My Job", *Newsweek*, 21 June 2008.
http://www.thedailybeast.com/newsweek/2008/06/21/there-s-no-year-that-i-didn-t-love-my-job.html

TEENAGE YEARS

Steve Levy, *Hackers: Heroes of the Computer Revolution: 25th Anniversary Edition* (Sebastopol, CA: O'Reilly Media, 2010).

TELEVISION

David Rensin, 'The Bill Gates Interview', *Playboy*, July 1994.

THINKING

John Emmerling, 'Gates-ian Ideas Work in Ad Biz', *Advertising Age*, 23 September 1996.

http://adage.com/article/news/forum-gates-ian-ideas-work-ad-biz-clear-direction-time-elements-winning-system-microsoft/77614

VACATION

Robert Slater, *Microsoft Rebooted: How Bill Gates and Steve Ballmer Reinvented Their Company* (New York: Portfolio, 2004).

WARREN BUFFETT

Oliver Burkeman, 'Bill Gates: I Don't Want to Be World's Richest Man', *Guardian*, 5 May 2006.
http://www.guardian.co.uk/media/2006/may/05/citynews.digitalmedia
'An Hour with Bill Gates,' *Charlie Rose Show*, 22 December 2008.
http://www.charlierose.com/download/transcript/10576
'Warren Buffett & Bill Gates: Keeping America Great', CNBC Town Hall Event transcript, Columbia University, 12 November 2009.
http://www.cnbc.com/id/33901003/CNBC_TRANSCRIPT_Warren_Buffett_Bill_Gates_Keeping_America_Great
'Bill Gates Keynote Speech: A Conversation with Bill Gates', San Jose State, San Jose, CA, 27 January 1998.
http://web.archive.org/web/20100909091356/http://www.microsoft.com/presspass/exec/billg/speeches/1998/sanjose.aspx
'Warren Buffett & Bill Gates: Keeping America Great', CNBC Town Hall Event transcript, Columbia University, 12 November 2009.
http://www.cnbc.com/id/33901003/CNBC_TRANSCRIPT_Warren_Buffett_Bill_Gates_Keeping_America_Great

WATCHING CHEMISTRY LECTURES

Todd Bishop and Tom Paulson, 'Gates Talks about Letting Go', *Seattle Post-Intelligencer*, 23 June 2008.
http://www.seattlepi.com/business/article/Q-A-Gates-talks-about-letting-go-the-future-and-1277371.php

WEALTH

Oliver Burkeman, 'Bill Gates: I Don't Want to Be World's Richest Man', *Guardian*, 5 May 2006.
http://www.guardian.co.uk/media/2006/may/05/citynews.digitalmedia
David Rensin, 'The Bill Gates Interview', *Playboy*, July 1994.

WHAT MAKES HIM MAD

Donny Deutsch, *The Big Idea*, CNBC, 8 May 2006.
http://adage.com/article/news/highlights-ms-summit/109042/

(HIS) WIFE

Barbara Walters, 'The Mind of Bill Gates', *20/20*, ABC, 30 January 1998.

WORK HABITS

'How I Work: Bill Gates', CNNMoney, 7 April 2006.
money.cnn.com/2006/03/30/news/newsmakers/gates_howiwork_fortune/

WORKING WITH HIS WIFE

Michael D Eisner and Aaron R Cohen, *Working Together: Why Great Partnerships Succeed* (New York: HarperBusiness, 2010).
Leonard Kniffel, *Reading with the Stars: A Celebration of Books and Libraries* (New York: Skyhorse Publishing, 2011).

WORLDVIEW

Steve Levy, *Hackers: Heroes of the Computer Revolution: 25th Anniversary Edition* (Sebastopol, CA: O'Reilly Media, 2010).
Walter Isaacson, 'In Search of the Real Bill Gates', *Time*, 13 January 1997.
http://www.time.com/time/magazine/article/0,9171,1120657,00.html
Bill Gates, *The Road Ahead* (New York: Viking, 1995).

ABOUT THE EDITOR

Lisa Rogak is the *New York Times* bestselling author of more than forty books on a variety of subjects, from popular culture to dogs. She has also written a number of biographies, including those of Stephen King, Shel Silverstein, Dan Brown, Dr Robert Atkins, Stephen Colbert and others. She lives in the Bay Area of northern California.

Her website is www.lisarogak.com.